Prolonged Exposure Therapy for PTSD

Teen Workbook

Kelly R. Chrestman • Eva Gilboa-Schechtman • Edna B. Foa

2009

Oxford University Press, Inc., publishes works that further
Oxford University's objective of excellence
in research, scholarship, and education.

Oxford New York
Auckland Cape Town Dar es Salaam Hong Kong Karachi
Kuala Lumpur Madrid Melbourne Mexico City Nairobi
New Delhi Shanghai Taipei Toronto

With offices in
Argentina Austria Brazil Chile Czech Republic France Greece
Guatemala Hungary Italy Japan Poland Portugal Singapore
South Korea Switzerland Thailand Turkey Ukraine Vietnam

Published by Oxford University Press, Inc.
198 Madison Avenue, New York, New York 10016

www.oup.com

ISBN 978-0-19-533173-8

Contents

Goals

- To understand the characteristics of posttraumatic stress disorder (PTSD)
- To learn about Prolonged Exposure Therapy for Adolescents (PE-A)
- To learn what the program will involve

What Is Posttraumatic Stress Disorder (PTSD)?

PTSD is an anxiety disorder that may develop after a trauma. The traumatic event can be experienced (for example, being attacked) or witnessed (for example, seeing someone else being attacked) and involves actual or perceived physical threat. The emotional response to the event is one of fear, helplessness, or horror. Teens with PTSD have three major types of symptoms:

1. Re-experiencing the trauma (for example, through memories or dreams)
2. Avoidance of trauma reminders (including efforts to avoid activities, people, or places that remind the person of the trauma)

3. Hyperarousal (difficulty sleeping, irritability, difficulty concentrating, hypervigilance, and exaggerated startled response)

These types of symptoms are very common right after traumatic events. But for most trauma survivors, the PTSD symptoms naturally decrease over time. However, for some people, the PTSD symptoms continue and interfere with daily life. If this is true in your case, this program, PE-A, can help.

What Is Prolonged Exposure Therapy for Adolescents (PE-A)?

PE-A is a treatment created especially for adolescents, people ages 13–18. It is based on an adult treatment called Prolonged Exposure (PE), but it has been modified to fit the lifestyle and preferences of teens. In PE-A, teens are helped to confront safe but anxiety-arousing situations in order to decrease their excessive fear and anxiety. You may already be familiar with the principles of exposure therapy. A classic example of exposure is the advice to a rider to "get back on the horse" after being thrown off. In doing so, the rider prevents her fear from growing out of control and overcomes her fear of being thrown again. The PE-A program includes two kinds of exposure:

- *Real-Life Experiments:* you will repeatedly face situations or activities that you are avoiding because they remind you of your traumatic experience and make you anxious or distressed
- *Recounting the Memory:* you will revisit the trauma in your imagination over and over again

Exposures are the core of the treatment. These techniques have helped many teens reduce anxiety and distress. Exposure is a powerful way for you to learn that the memories of the trauma and the situations or activities that are associated with these memories are not the same as the trauma itself. You will learn that it is safe to remember your trauma and experience the trauma reminders. As you face these situations and memories over and over again, you will find out that remembering the trauma and facing trauma reminders do not cause harm and as a result your anxiety and distress during these situations will go down. Ultimately, this treatment will help you reclaim your life from PTSD.

What Is Emotional Processing Theory?

PE-A also helps teens *emotionally process* their traumatic experiences. By confronting memories and situations associated with the trauma, you will have a chance to digest what happened to you. You will learn to challenge your fears and beliefs about anxiety. You and your therapist will discuss how you are thinking and feeling about the trauma and how your thoughts and feelings change over time. This "processing" will help change your fear structure so you will no longer be afraid of situations and memories that are not actually dangerous. As you continue to practice exposures and process the trauma, you will become more confident in your ability to cope.

Outline of This Treatment Program

In all, you will attend 10–15 weekly or twice-weekly treatment sessions that are generally 60–90 minutes each. You and your therapist will be working together in session to overcome your PTSD; you will also have homework to do in between sessions. Your therapist will discuss with you how your parents, family, or others close to you can support you during treatment.

The treatment is organized into units that will be covered in order as you work your way through the treatment. A unit represents a specific topic area or treatment technique.

Some units are short and will take only one session to complete. Other units will take several sessions to complete.

Use of This Workbook and Audio Recordings

This workbook includes a chapter for each unit of treatment. Each chapter lists the goals for the unit and gives an overview of what will happen in the sessions. It explains the treatment techniques and how you will use them. It includes homework instructions and all the necessary forms. Your therapist may also provide you with an audio recording of each session to review as part of your homework. After the first session, you will also receive a recording to help you practice relaxed breathing at home. During the "Recounting the Memory" unit, you will be given additional audio recordings of yourself recounting your traumatic memory in session. These recordings are for you to listen to once a day at home.

Reading the workbook, completing the exercises, and listening to the tapes will help you get the most out of this treatment. PE-A is designed to get you in touch with your emotions and reactions to trauma. This is often painful, especially at first. This is why it is best to do PE-A with the help of a trained therapist who will be there to help you through it. Therapy can be challenging at times, but it is important to stick with it. Remember, you are on your way to taking your life back!

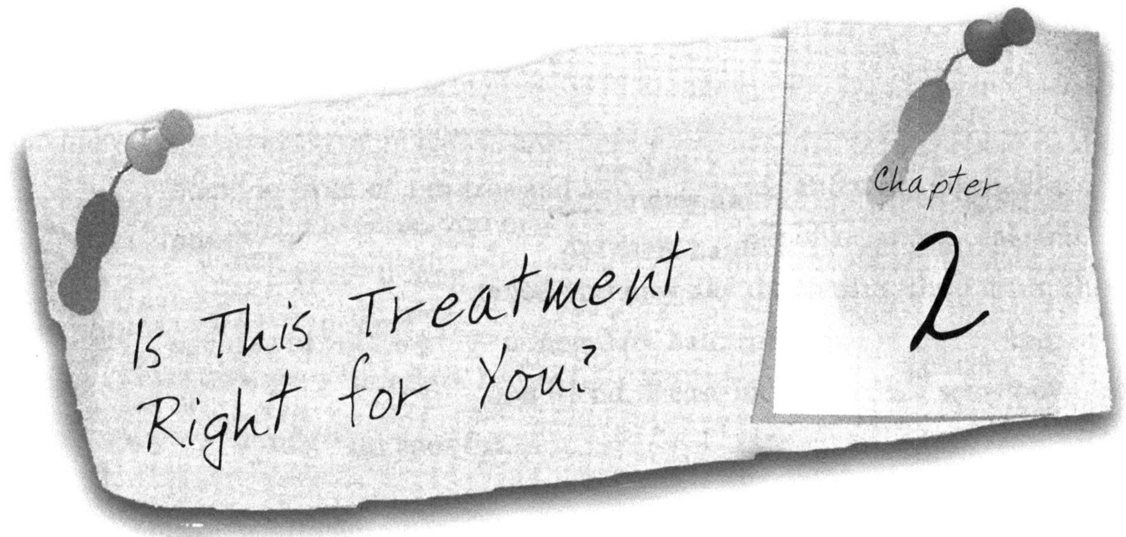

Goals

- To make a list of life domains that have been disrupted as a result of the trauma
- To think and talk about potential benefits of your participation in therapy
- To think and talk about possible costs of your participation in therapy
- To think and talk about what might be difficult about participating in therapy
- To help you decide if the treatment is right for you

Overview

This unit is designed to help you weigh the pros and cons of starting this treatment program. Your therapist will help you think about your life before and after the trauma. Together, you will evaluate the changes that have occurred. You will find out the benefits of reducing symptoms, such as sleeping better or feeling less afraid. You will also discuss what you may lose as a result of reducing your PTSD symptoms. For example, you may have to return to some chores or responsibilities that you were allowed to avoid because you were having symptoms of PTSD. If there are things that might interfere with your completing treatment, such as feeling ashamed about being in therapy or difficulty getting family or friends to support your decision to come to treatment, your therapist will brainstorm with you about how to manage the situation.

Your Motivation for Therapy

To help you think about your motivation for treatment, answer the following questions. Try to be honest with yourself, even if it means that you do not feel very excited about the treatment. This is just the beginning of the discussion and there are many things that can affect your feelings about treatment. You and your therapist will return to these questions again after you have had a chance to review the things that affect your motivation in more detail.

1. Why did you decide to seek therapy *now*?

____

____

2. How do you feel about the idea of beginning therapy?

____

____

3. On a scale of 0–10, where 0 represents "not at all interested" and 10 represents "very interested," how would you rank your level of interest in this current therapy?

0 1 2 3 4 5 6 7 8 9 10

4. What does the number you chose mean to you?

____

____

Disruption of Life Domains

Trauma affects many different areas, or domains, of life. Some areas may be affected more than others for you. Use the Life Domains form to help you think about how different areas of your life have been affected by the trauma. As you think about each area, try to recall how things were before the trauma and how things have changed since the trauma. Be sure to think about positive as well as negative changes. Also think about how you expected things to be now and how they really are. For example, you may not have gotten your driver's license before the trauma, and now, you are too scared to get it even though you have reached the legal age to get your license. In this example, you expected a change that *didn't* happen.

LIFE DOMAINS FORM

For each life domain, describe what your life was like before and after the trauma. Be sure to list positive as well as negative changes.

Emotional health (anxiety, depression, anger, shame, self-confidence, self-esteem, ability to relax):

Before: ____________________

____

After: ____________________

____

Physical health (fitness, diet, exercise, sleep habits, tiredness, injury, and illness):

Before: ____________________

____

After: ____________________

____

Leisure (friends, extracurricular activities, trips):

Before: ____________________

____

After: ____________________

____

School (grades, teachers' assessments, homework, level of concentration):

Before: ____________________

____

After: ____________________

____

continued

____

Relationship with family members (fights, level of sharing, sense of closeness):

Before: ______________________________

____

After: ______________________________

____

Relationship with close friends (fights, level of sharing, sense of closeness):

Before: ______________________________

____

After: ______________________________

____

Social status in class/social circles (popularity, feel appreciated, people turn to for help):

Before: ______________________________

____

After: ______________________________

____

Independence (for example, going places alone):

Before: ______________________________

____

After: ______________________________

____

Use of drugs and/or alcohol:

Before: ______________________________

____

continued

____

After: ____

____

Body image (how do you feel about the way you look?):

Before: ____

____

After: ____

____

Sources of pleasure (music, sports, hobbies):

Before: ____

____

After: ____

____

Are there other things that your friends or other people your age are able to do that you do not do at the present time?

Social outings: ____

____

School: ____

____

Hobbies: ____

____

Travel/Transportation: ____

____

Other: ____

____

____

Potential Benefits of Therapy

The Life Domains form should have helped you to focus in on the areas of your life that were affected by the trauma. What were the biggest changes? The most disruptive? The most disappointing? The scariest? Are there areas that stand out for you above the others? Did any of your answers come as a surprise to you? Many people do not realize how much the trauma has affected their everyday lives because they have been focusing so much on their symptoms, such as fear and anxiety. We often say that PTSD shrinks your life because so many important and fulfilling aspects of life are affected by the symptoms of PTSD, particularly the avoidance. Does it seem that your life has "shrunk" since the trauma?

Treatment for PTSD can help you reduce or eliminate the symptoms of PTSD and it can also help you to get your life back. What were you hoping to gain from treatment? Are the symptoms your main concern? Are there life domains that have been changed in unexpected and disappointing ways? The following questions may help you identify changes you would like to make.

1. What would you like to change in your life now?

   ____

   ____

2. What do you wish you could do at the end of therapy or in three months time?

   ____

   ____

3. What would you like to do when you are older?

   ____

   ____

4. What do you think you need to do to meet these goals?

____

____

Potential Obstacles to Therapy

Therapy requires time and effort. At times, you may feel that your level of distress increases before it decreases. Think about what you know about yourself and your lifestyle. Are you very busy with lots of extracurricular activities? Are your family and friends supportive of your starting treatment? Are you having difficulty keeping up in school? Are you worried you won't have time to do all your treatment assignments? Are you afraid treatment will be too painful or scary? List things that may make it difficult to continue in therapy:

____

____

____

It is important to address these obstacles so you can successfully complete treatment. Often, patients are able to prioritize or rearrange some of their activities for the time they are in treatment. Remember, treatment does not last forever, it is actually for a relatively short period of time.

Your therapist will help you problem solve around these obstacles. If you have tried therapy in the past, be sure to discuss with your therapist how this current treatment may be similar or different.

Potential Costs of Therapy

Having a condition, such as PTSD, may have brought about positive as well as negative changes in your life. For example, your parents or teachers may be more flexible with you. If you get better you may lose these benefits. Knowing this can make it hard to fully commit to treatment, especially if you are not sure that treatment can really help. The following questions will help you identify any positive changes that have occurred and how willing you are to give them up.

1. Are there aspects of your life that have actually changed for the better since the trauma?

   ____

   ____

2. How important are these positive changes to you?

   ____

   ____

3. How important is it to you that you reduce your PTSD symptoms?

   ____

   ____

Summarizing the Pros and Cons

Any kind of therapy may be difficult and demanding. Summarizing the pros and cons can help you decide whether the effort of therapy is in fact worthwhile for you. Complete the Pros and Cons of Therapy form (see Figure 2.1 for an example). Think about the obstacles, the difficulties, and the demands. Do you have time to devote to treatment? Would treatment make your life harder? In the short run? In the long run? Would you

Pros	Cons
Improved sleep—more energy for school and friends	Will have to attend school regularly when symptoms improve
Less irritability—get along better with family and friends	Will need to spend one hour per day doing treatment activities
Less avoidance of doing things by myself—free to ride the bus and walk instead of waiting for car rides	Will be more effort to walk to school if parents no longer drive me after my symptoms improve

Figure 2.1 Example of Completed Pros and Cons of Therapy Form

have to give up anything if you got better (for example, free time, special treatment, or extra help at school)? Then think about how therapy might change things for the better for you. Do the benefits outweigh costs? Does it make sense for you to start treatment now? Is it better to wait until a later time? The choice to enter treatment is yours. Your therapist will help you think about the pros and cons so that you can feel your decision to enter treatment makes sense and is in your best interest.

Homework

- ✎ Review this chapter for homework.
- ✎ Listen to the recording of the session.
- ✎ Review Life Domains form for accuracy and add any other items that come up during the week.
- ✎ Review Pros and Cons of Therapy form for accuracy and add any other items that come up during the week.

Pros and Cons of Therapy

Pros	Cons

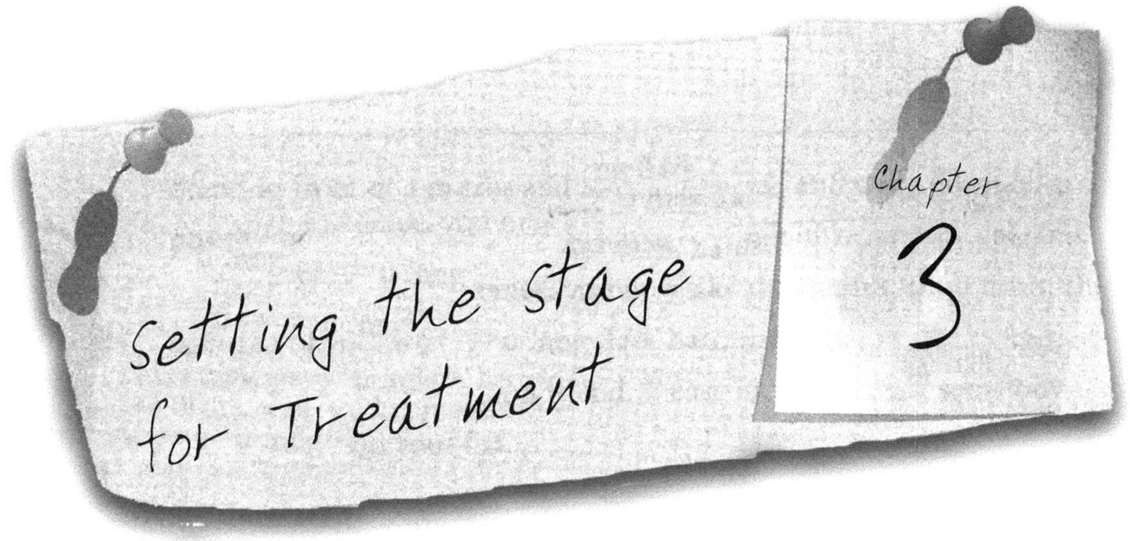

Goals

- To understand your right to confidentiality and privacy in therapy
- To decide how involved your parents will be in your therapy
- To make a crisis coping plan if necessary
- To address other problems if necessary

Overview

This unit will help you set the stage for successful treatment. You will discuss with your therapist a topic that is very important for most teenagers, your privacy. You will discuss how this works when you start treatment, including how much your parents will and won't be involved in your treatment. If you identified obstacles to treatment in the last unit you may work on a plan to get around them. If suicidal thoughts are part of your symptoms, you will work with your therapist on a plan for dealing with them during treatment. Your therapist will most likely speak to you first and then to your parents to get their take on things. Finally you, your parents, and your therapist will all meet together to iron out the details.

Confidentiality and Privacy

You have the right to confidentiality in therapy. This means that, with a few exceptions, the content of your meetings are private. Your parents, however, also have a right to know about your therapy and how it is working. Your therapist will negotiate with you and your parents about what information to share with them. Your therapist will keep your personal details confidential. Of course, you are free to discuss whatever you like with your parents at any time. However, you need to know that by law your therapist must share information about you when there is a good chance of harm to you or to someone else. Again, this does not mean your therapist will share personal details, but he or she will need to share enough information to serve your best interests. For example, if you were planning to harm yourself, or if someone else was harming you, your therapist would share information to keep you safe. Your therapist might also share information if you were engaging in extremely dangerous behavior such as drinking and driving. When your life or your safety is at stake, it is important to have all the support you can get, so you, your therapist, and your parents will need to work together on any issues of danger.

Parental Involvement

In deciding how much you want your parents to be involved, think about your relationship with each of them. Are you able to talk about your feelings with either of them? Your parents probably have their own strengths and weaknesses, so you will want to take advantage of what your parents are good at. Is one or both of your parents able to encourage you when you feel anxious or when you doubt yourself? Are they good at helping you solve problems? That skill will come in handy if you need to find a creative way to confront something.

Your therapist can play a big role in helping your parents support you in the best way. If you are comfortable with their involvement, your parents' job will be to give you support and help as you progress through therapy. Most people are unaware of the particular techniques and skills you will learn in this treatment. Your therapist can teach your parents how to help you use these skills and how to stand back and let you do things yourself when you need to do so.

Your therapist will also get information from your parents about their preferences. Then, you, your therapist, and your parents will negotiate an agreement about how your parents are to be involved in your treatment. Depending on the agreement, your parents may participate in some sessions and/or homework activities. Regardless of how much your parents participate in your treatment, there are several handouts your therapist may give them to help them understand what you are going through.

Planning for Crises

Many teenagers have thoughts about dying or harming themselves after experiencing a trauma such as you have. For some, these thoughts happen once in a while. For others, the thoughts can be almost constant, involving detailed plans. Some teens have attempted suicide in the past, and still think about doing it some time in the future. While this is not unusual, it is important that you talk about those kinds of thoughts as part of your therapy. If you have suicidal thoughts, intentions, or plans, your therapist will help you come up with a plan for coping with and overcoming them. This plan may also include dealing with risky or self-injurious behaviors. You will have a chance to discuss the plan with your parents and agree on how you will cope as a family.

Identifying Other Problems

There may be other issues that affect your ability to participate in therapy. These may include symptoms like depression, difficulties at school, or family changes. You may have other commitments that get in the way (for example, an after-school job or extracurricular activities). Your therapist will help you identify these issues and come up with some possible solutions. Together, you will decide how to address each problem during the course of therapy.

Homework

- ✎ Review this chapter for homework.
- ✎ Listen to the recording of the session.
- ✎ Review crisis coping plan if you made one.
- ✎ Address other problems as discussed in session.

Goals

- To learn about the treatment program
- To learn how you will face your fears
- To learn a breathing exercise that can help you feel calmer
- To gather information about the trauma
- To complete the Secret Weapons exercise

Overview

Over the course of this treatment, you will be asked to change things that you have been doing to cope with the trauma and that prevent you from getting better. For example, you may be asked to face safe situations that make you scared rather than avoiding them. Making these kinds of changes can be very hard. It is much easier when you understand the "Hows," "Whys," and "Whats." During this unit, your therapist will help you understand *how* this treatment works, *why* it is important to face your fears, and *what* techniques you need to use to help you face your fears. As part of the treatment planning, your therapist will be asking you questions to gather details about the trauma. In this section, you will also begin learning new skills that will be helpful in overcoming your fears. In session, you will practice a breathing exercise to help you feel calmer.

Introduction to the Treatment

After experiencing a trauma, it is natural to feel afraid, sad, ashamed, angry, or a combination of these and other uncomfortable feelings. Right after a trauma, many people have trouble talking about what happened to them. They also find that they want to avoid things that might remind them of the trauma. For some people, the scared and sad feelings will begin to get better after a while. For others, and maybe for you, the uncomfortable feelings seem to stay or even get worse over time. Unwanted thoughts about the trauma pop up unexpectedly, even when you are trying very hard *not* to think about it. Some people find that they have a hard time doing things that used to be easy for them. For example, they may have trouble going to school, sleeping in their own beds at night, taking public transportation, walking around in shopping malls, or doing other outside activities. Some even lose interest in socializing and fun activities. Sometimes it can seem like life will never be the same again. This program will help you get past your fears and get back to your life.

How You Will Face Your Fears

It is normal to want to escape or avoid things that are painful and upsetting. You may find yourself avoiding situations, memories, thoughts, and feelings related to the trauma. In the short run, this seems like a good plan because it helps you feel better temporarily, but it actually makes things worse in the long run. Avoidance makes it more difficult to get past the post-trauma difficulties that some people experience. It also prevents you from returning to everyday activities.

In this program, you will face situations and memories you have been avoiding. This will give you the chance to process, or discuss and think about, the traumatic experience in a way that helps you get past your reactions to it. For example, you may be avoiding trauma-related situations that make you feel bad or anxious but that are actually safe in real life. By avoiding these situations you do not give yourself the chance to realize that these situations are safe. This is why avoidance keeps you from getting over your fear of being in these situations. Unless you face the situations, you may continue to believe that they are dangerous and that your anxiety will never go away. However, if you face these situations you will find out that they are not actually dangerous. You will also find out that your anxiety will become less and less intense as you get used to facing and staying in those situations. As a result, your symptoms will get better.

The same is true for facing painful memories. Facing upsetting memories is not dangerous, but it may be uncomfortable. This is because remembering brings back the old feelings that were there when the trauma happened. If you face and process the memory, the intensity of the old feelings will gradually weaken. Eventually, you will be able to remember the trauma without feeling so bad.

Trauma Interview

At some point near the beginning of treatment, your therapist will want to ask you for more information about the trauma. You may have already discussed some of the details with your therapist or with others before you decided to start treatment, but your therapist will want to hear the full story from you first hand.

You will describe what you have been through, how it has affected you, and how your life has changed as a result of the trauma you experienced. You will be asked to talk generally about what happened to you before, during, and after the trauma, including what you were thinking and how you felt. It may be difficult for you to talk about certain things, but you should try your best to give as much detail as possible. Remember, the memory cannot hurt you today as the trauma did in the past, and this information is important for doing exposures later.

Techniques to Overcome Fears: Recounting the Memory and Real-Life Experiments

There are two techniques you will learn in this treatment that will help you face fearful situations and memories. The first technique is *recounting the memory*. In the safety of your therapist's office, you will repeatedly tell the story of what happened just as you remember it. Your therapist will be there to support and help you. Each time you recount the memory, you will add as many details, thoughts, and feelings as you can recall. Recounting the memory in this way helps you to think about, discuss, and process what happened. The feelings that have been bothering you will begin to feel less intense and painful.

The second technique is *real-life experiments*. You will be asked to gradually begin to face situations that you have been avoiding since the trauma. These situations may remind you, directly or indirectly, of the trauma, or they may seem unsafe to you because of your experiences. As you practice the real-life experiments, you will begin to learn that the situations you are facing are actually fairly safe. With each repetition of an experiment, your fear will decrease. Real-life experiments will help you to start doing all the things that you have stopped doing since your trauma because you have been feeling afraid.

Negative Thoughts and Beliefs

Unhelpful, disturbing thoughts and beliefs may be another reason why you may feel anxious and upset. After a trauma, lots of people start thinking that the world is a dangerous and disappointing place. They may also think that many people—including themselves—are disappointing. Because of this, even safe situations may seem dangerous or unpredictable. Some people even think that they are weak or out of control. They may feel unable to deal with normal daily stresses. Some may also blame themselves for their behavior during the trauma. Or they may feel guilty or ashamed over the fact that they developed difficulties after the trauma. They may start feeling ashamed about themselves. If you are having these kinds of thoughts and feelings, you may not want to talk with anyone about what happened to you.

During treatment, you will learn to identify negative thoughts when they happen. You can then examine if they are realistic or helpful. This is important because many times these thoughts make PTSD symptoms worse and dealing with everyday life more difficult. Real-life experiments and recounting the memory will help you correct unrealistic and unhelpful thoughts. These techniques will improve your everyday coping by providing you with tools to realistically evaluate the following:

- whether a situation is in fact dangerous
- whether you are able to cope with it

Support and Teamwork

You and your therapist are going to work hard together during the next few months. The goal is to help you get on with your life. As you discuss the trauma and your reactions to the trauma, you may find yourself experiencing discomfort. Outside of therapy, you may even experience a temporary worsening of your problems. Your therapist will be available to help you when needed. You, your therapist, and your parents will work together as a team in order to help you and your family to overcome the trauma.

Breathing Retraining

During the session, you will learn a breathing exercise to help you begin to feel better. The purpose of this exercise is the following:

- To slow down your breathing
- To breathe in less air
- With practice, feel calmer

Very often, when people become scared or upset, they feel like they need more air. They may start to breathe in and out very quickly, causing them to get too much air. This is called **hyperventilation**. It can feel very uncomfortable. It may even make a person feel anxious or scared. This may have happened to you before if you have ever breathed in too much air.

Breathing in and out really fast tricks your body into thinking you need to run away or fight. What you really need to do is to slow down your breathing and take in less air. If you practice this kind of slower breathing often, you will begin to feel calmer.

Breathing Instructions

1. Take a normal breath in through your nose with your mouth closed.
2. Breathe out slowly with your mouth closed.

3. On exhaling, silently say to yourself the word **CALM** or **RELAX** very slowly, for example, *c-a-a-a-a-a-l-m* or *r-e-e-e-e-e-e-l-a-x*.

4. Count slowly to 4 and then take the next inhalation.

5. Practice this exercise three times a day, for 10–15 minutes each time.

Many people find that this exercise, called "relaxed breathing," is pretty helpful in stressful situations of all kinds. We want you to use it to help yourself feel calmer. That way you won't be so tempted to escape when you are confronted with a difficult situation during the therapy. Breathing in this relaxed manner can give you a few seconds to think, and decide to stay rather than to avoid. You may still feel anxious and want to leave the situation. Relaxed breathing won't take away all your fears, but it may make it more likely that you will think about what you are doing and resist the urge to avoid. This will be very important in the next sessions, when you begin doing real-life experiments and recounting the memory.

One more hint about relaxed breathing: It almost always gets better with practice. Many people find that it is not very relaxing when they first try it out, because they are busy trying to count and remember the steps. The more you practice, the easier it gets and the more second nature it becomes. So don't give up on the breathing if it does not seem to help at first. Your skill will likely improve if you practice, and you will have one more tool to help you combat your fears.

Secret Weapons Exercise

Therapy can seem hard at first. No one wants to talk about things that make them upset. Fortunately, it gets easier with practice. Think about other things you have learned to do that were hard at first, but became easier with practice. Remember, you are capable of doing something hard or scary, learning from it, and doing it well. Also, there are many people who will help you along the way.

The Secret Weapons form can help you assess the resources you have to learn to cope with and conquer PTSD symptoms. The form covers the following three areas:

1. *Skills and talents* include anything you can do (sing, dance, write stories, draw, ride a bike, etc.) that demonstrates your persistence, your ability to learn, your courage, or other good qualities.
2. *Experiences and accomplishments* include chores, good grades, awards, recovery from an illness or a broken bone, passing a grade, getting through a tough time in your life, or any experience that shows the reward of hard work, even if the experience was not pleasant at the time.
3. *Allies and assets* include people such as teachers, parents, or friends, and resources such as school, religious organizations, or clubs, as well as religious figures, prayers, God, or anything that helps you feel supported and cared for.

Secret Weapons

Skills & Talents	Experiences & Accomplishments	Allies & Assets

Homework

- ✎ Review this chapter for homework.
- ✎ Listen to the recordings of the session and the breathing exercise.
- ✎ Complete Secret Weapons form if assigned.
- ✎ Practice the breathing exercise 3 times per day.

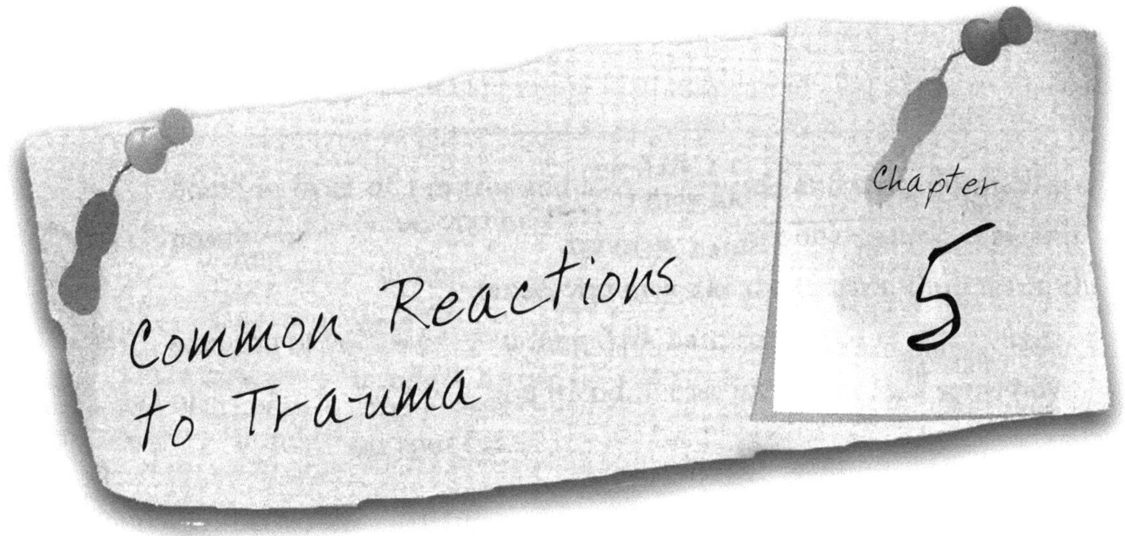

Goals

- To learn about common reactions to trauma
- To identify your own reactions to trauma

Overview

A traumatic event is an extremely distressing life experience. It makes sense that it often creates intense emotional and physical reactions. Everyone reacts strongly to a trauma shortly after the event. With most people, these reactions (sometimes called symptoms) will decrease over time. Sometimes, however, these reactions do not go away and continue to cause difficulties for the person. This is called a posttraumatic stress reaction. In this unit, you and your therapist will discuss common reactions to trauma and identify which ones you have experienced.

Fear and Anxiety

The most common reactions to trauma are fear and anxiety, which are natural reactions to danger. When we are in a dangerous situation, an internal alarm system is triggered. The purpose of this system is to warn us and help us react in the best way to protect ourselves. This "alarm system" triggers certain reactions in our bodies (faster heartbeat, sweating, etc.) that help us focus on the danger that we must defend ourselves against. The alarm system also exists in animals. Think of the squirrel that scampers up a tree when you walk near it in the park, the cat that hisses in the presence of a threatening dog, or the rabbit that freezes when hearing a twig snap in the distance. In times of danger, this system helps us flee the situation, fight against it, or freeze. These are natural reactions in the face of danger.

This alarm system may also be activated by *triggers* or *cues*, which are related to the trauma but are not in themselves dangerous. When this happens, the reactions to trauma and danger continue to happen long after the traumatic experience has ended, and they get in the way of daily life. The more you pay attention to your anxiety, the more you can identify the triggers or cues that cause the anxiety. Sometimes, the anxiety that appears to come out of nowhere is actually triggered by something that reminds you of the trauma. Things that may trigger anxiety are sights, smells, noises, or situations that remind you of the trauma. For example, a person who had experienced a traffic accident may feel sudden anxiety and not understand the cause of it. If he pays attention, he will notice a distant screech of car brakes or a siren, and recognize these triggers as the cause of the anxiety.

Feeling on Edge

Feeling on edge is another common reaction. After a traumatic event, many people feel jittery and on edge almost all the time. For example, your body may feel hyper. Or you may have a fast heartbeat and breathe quickly. You may be cautious and jumpy, startled easily, and react strongly to minor events such as the noise of a car.

As a result of continuous jumpiness, some people develop concentration difficulties, trouble falling asleep, and restless sleep. Constantly feeling on edge may also cause irritability and anger, especially if the person does not get enough sleep.

Re-experiencing

Sometimes people who have experienced a trauma may *re-experience* it. This happens when thoughts or feelings about the trauma pop into your mind. A reminder of the event can trigger these thoughts, or they may seem to come out of nowhere.

Flashbacks

An extreme form of re-experiencing is a flashback. Flashbacks are very vivid images, which give the feeling that the event is taking place in the here and now. For example, you may feel as though the assault is actually taking place in the present moment. You may even feel that you actually see or hear some of what had happened. Sometimes, the flashback can be so powerful that you may feel that the trauma occurs over and over again.

Nightmares

Some people also re-experience the trauma through dreams or nightmares. The traumatic event is so horrific and different from daily life that it is difficult for the mind to organize the event and put it away. Dreams are one way the mind uses to go over the event again and again as it tries to understand or digest it.

Avoidance

Many people try to avoid anything that triggers feelings of distress, fear, and anxiety. They find themselves avoiding all kinds of situations, places, or people that remind them of the trauma. For example, you may avoid approaching the place where the trauma happened.

Another type of avoidance is related to thoughts and feelings regarding the trauma. Many people actively try not to recall the trauma, not to talk about it, and not to feel emotions connected with it. They may even experience difficulty remembering certain parts of the event.

Emotional Numbness

Sometimes people who have experienced a trauma have trouble feeling anything at all. This is called *emotional numbness*. Following the trauma, this lack of feelings may help you feel less fear and anxiety, but it also prevents the experience of positive feelings. So you end up feeling less happy, satisfied, or loving. You may notice that you don't feel as close to people. Your friends may not seem to understand you in the same way they used to. You may feel *detached* or cutoff from others without really understanding why.

Anger

Some people also feel a very strong sense of anger after a trauma. This anger may be directed toward the traumatic event and the people involved in it, but it can also be directed toward people in general. Sometimes anger is directed toward friends and family because you think that they are not able to understand what you are going through.

Guilt and Shame

Many people feel guilty and ashamed for things that they did, or did not do, during the trauma. They may blame themselves for what happened by saying things like, "I should have been less afraid," or "I should have known that such a thing would happen." They may also feel guilty for the problems they have been experiencing since the trauma, and because their symptoms have created difficulties for their family and friends.

You may also feel ashamed if you reacted differently from what you expected of yourself during the trauma (for example, crying or freezing on the spot). You may also feel ashamed about the problems you are experiencing now as a result of the trauma. This can be especially hard if the people close to you are critical of you as well.

Feelings of Losing Control

Sometimes during trauma, a person feels as though he has no control over his feelings, his body, and his life. Sometimes, the feeling of lack of control may be so powerful and scary that the person may believe that he is "going crazy" or "losing his sanity." These kinds of thoughts are common and are *not* a sign that you are really going crazy. The intense emotions and experiences brought on by the trauma are a normal response to extreme stress.

Changes of Perception

Sometimes, people's beliefs about themselves change following a trauma. You may say to yourself that you must be a "bad person" because bad things happened to you, or "if I were not so weak and stupid this would not have happened to me," or "I should have been braver." Your opinions about the world and about other people may change for the worse as well. If you thought before the trauma that the world is a safe place, you may now feel that the world is a dangerous place and that you cannot trust other people.

Depression

Some people begin to feel helpless and hopeless about their ability to recover and feel good again. It may seem as though nothing is fun anymore. They may believe there is nothing worth living for, and that their plans for the future are no longer important. Feelings of sadness, grief, and depression are common reactions to trauma. In fact, many people with PTSD also suffer from symptoms of depression. These thoughts and feelings can lead some people to think they would be better off dead. They may even think of harming themselves or committing suicide.

Understanding Your Reactions to Trauma

These are some of the most common reactions teenagers have after a trauma, but there are other reactions that you may have had because your experience was unique in some ways, as is every traumatic experience. What is important to understand is that your reactions make sense given the traumatic event that happened to you. More importantly, your reactions can become less intense and more manageable with treatment. You may experience certain reactions more strongly than other people, and some reactions you may not experience at all. Regardless of whether you experience only a few, or a great many of the reactions that were described earlier, this treatment program can help you recover. You can then return to doing the things that are important to you.

Homework

- ✎ Review this chapter for homework.
- ✎ Listen to the recording of the session.
- ✎ Complete Common Reactions to Trauma form.

Common Reactions to Trauma

Identify which reactions to trauma you have experienced and record details of your experience.

Fear and Anxiety:
Feeling on Edge:
Re-experiencing:
Avoidance:
Emotional Numbness:
Anger:
Guilt and Shame:
Feelings of Losing Control:
Changes of Perception:
Symptoms of Depression:
Other Reactions:

Goals

- To understand how avoidance is related to PTSD symptoms
- To build a hierarchy of real-life experiments
- To practice real-life experiments

Overview

In this unit you will learn more about how avoidance keeps your PTSD symptoms strong and intense. You will also learn about a technique called *real-life experiments*. These "experiments" will help you start facing those situations you have been avoiding. You and your therapist will then begin creating a plan to start facing those situations in real life, arranging the situations from easier ones to more difficult ones. You will be facing each of these situations one by one, like climbing a ladder step by step. By repeatedly confronting these situations, you will get used to handling them and overcome your fears.

The Problem With Avoidance

It is normal to want to avoid situations, feelings, and thoughts that remind you of the trauma. This is because being reminded of the trauma brings back the same unpleasant feelings you felt during the trauma. Pushing away the thoughts and staying away from the reminders of trauma can help you to feel a little bit better in the short run, but in the long run, the fear will remain strong and may even get worse with continued avoidance. You start to do less and less as time goes by, even missing out on important things. For example, some teenagers no longer go out with friends, drive to places, or sleep alone in bed. This kind of restriction on your independence or social life may cause you to feel even more sad and lonely.

How Do Real-life Experiments Work?

As long as you continue to avoid situations that remind you of your trauma, you will continue to strengthen your habit of overcoming anxiety and fear by avoiding or escaping these situations. Also, as long as you continue to avoid the situations you will continue to believe that something bad will happen to you if you stop avoiding. As you confront your fears, you will learn that the scary situations are not really dangerous. You will do this through real-life experiments. These are like "field experiments," where you practice the different situations you have been avoiding in order to see what happens. As you repeatedly confront situations that you have been avoiding and find that nothing bad happens, you gather "evidence" that the situations are safe and it is not necessary to avoid them. If you do not confront the situations you will continue to believe that the situations are dangerous and you will never get the chance to correct your beliefs.

When you come across a situation you usually avoid, you probably feel anxious and fearful at first. For example, your heart beats fast, your palms are sweaty, you feel a

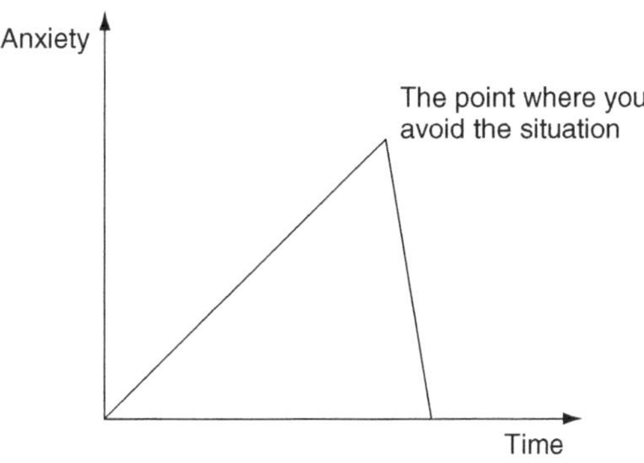

Figure 6.1 Avoidance Reduces Anxiety in the Short Run

tremble, and you want to leave the situation immediately. If you then avoid or escape the situation, your anxiety will probably decrease immediately (see Figure 6.1). However, avoiding or escaping will not make your difficulties and problems go away and you will continue to suffer. This is because avoidance does not allow you to learn that if you stay long enough in the situation your anxiety will decrease. You also will not get the chance to discover that the situation is actually not dangerous. You conclude wrongly that "you have saved yourself" from something terrible by avoiding or escaping. As a result, the next time you enter such a situation, your anxiety level will be high again and you will run away again. In this way, the cycle of avoidance will continue.

If instead of leaving, you stay in the situation, you will find that, much to your surprise, your anxiety begins to decrease after a while. It is important to remember that the learning process is a gradual one. In the first exposure, your anxiety may only decrease a little bit or not at all. But the more times you practice, the less anxiety you will feel. See Figure 6.2 and note that while the peak anxiety in the first exposure is still high, each subsequent peak gets smaller and smaller. Eventually, your anxiety will not even peak, but you will react to the situation that used to be scary with a calm and confident feeling. You will learn that your anxiety in the situation is temporary and will go away with repeated exposure. This is called **habituation**.

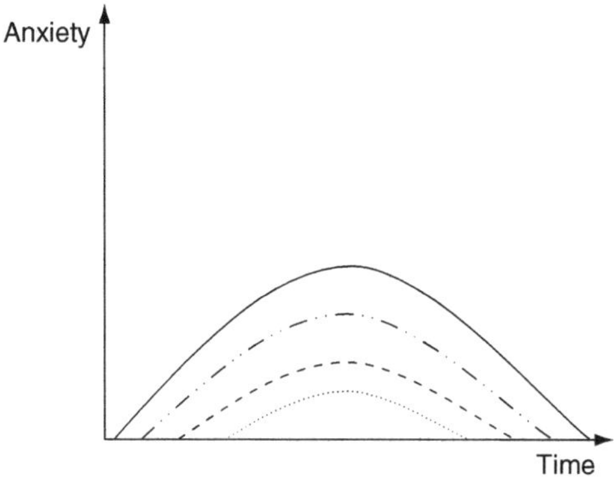

Figure 6.2 Anxiety Habituates With Successive Exposures

As you face your fears, you will begin to feel better about yourself and your ability to overcome your PTSD symptoms. You will begin to be able to do the things you enjoyed doing in the past but had stopped doing because of the trauma. In short, you will begin the process of getting your life back.

Introduction to Real-life Experiments

In doing real-life experiments, you and your therapist will be using a method similar to the one in the following story.

> *Once there was a little boy digging in the sand near the ocean's edge when a big wave came in and washed over him. He got very upset and scared. He cried and wanted to go home. The next day, he didn't want to go to the beach at all.*
>
> *To help him get rid of his fear his mother took him for walks on the beach for the next few days. At first they would walk on the dry sand away from the water. She would hold his hand and gradually they walked closer and closer to the water. By the end of the week, the little boy was able to walk in the water alone. With*

practice and encouragement, he overcame his fear of the water and was able to enjoy the beach again.

Real-life Experiments Hierarchy

Just as the little boy overcame his fears, so will you overcome your fears. Together, you and your therapist will prepare a list of situations you have been avoiding. Some will be very difficult and others will be easier for you. Practicing the real-life experiments will be like climbing a ladder. You will start with the least difficult situations—these are like the lowest steps on a ladder. The next steps will be higher and more difficult, but you will climb them one at a time from lowest to highest. With time and practice you will be able to conquer your fear and start to enjoy many situations again.

Stress Thermometer

Before you begin to create your list of avoided situations for your real-life experiments, you will need to come up with a way of rating your anxiety. This will help you and your therapist be able to communicate accurately about how anxious you are during your experiments. The stress thermometer is a personalized technique used to measure how upsetting or scary or sad a situation makes you feel. First, you and your therapist will come up with real examples from your life that correspond to the different levels of anxiety. You will write in the real-life examples from your past on the Stress Thermometer form in this chapter to serve as "anchors" along the scale.

A "10" on the stress thermometer is a feeling so upsetting; it's the worst you have ever felt in your life, and a "0" is when you are not feeling upset at all. At "10," you might have a racing heart, trembling, upset stomach, and breathing problems. It is an extreme and intense experience. At "0," you would be breathing normally, feeling just fine and relaxed. A "5," of course, is somewhere between. Perhaps you would feel your heart quicken, or be startled for a moment. You may feel anxious, but still able to be in control and cope.

Remember that each person's stress thermometer is unique. A situation that is a "10" for you might be no problem for someone else, and vice versa. The important thing is to come up with examples that are meaningful to you so you will easily remember them when you are comparing your current level of anxiety to the stress thermometer markings.

After you and your therapist have built your hierarchy using the Real-Life Experiments Step-by-Step form, you will rate the level of anxiety associated with each item on the list using the stress thermometer. You will also use the stress thermometer to rate your anxiety when you recount the memory of the trauma in the next unit.

Stress Thermometer

In the spaces provided, write real-life examples that correspond to that level of anxiety.

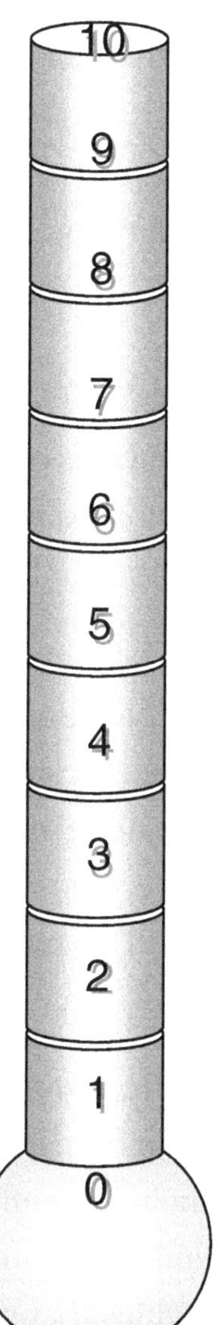

10. ______________________________________

5. ______________________________________

0. ______________________________________

Types of Situations for Your Real-Life Experiments

You and your therapist will work together to identify situations that you have been avoiding due to your PTSD symptoms. These situations will be recorded on the Real-Life Experiments Step-by-Step form. See Figure 6.3 for an example of a completed hierarchy.

You will be asked to rate how much anxiety and distress you think you would feel in each situation using the stress thermometer. You will get a chance to take the hierarchy home to add additional items to the list.

There are three main types of situations that you should consider for real-life experiments:

1. *Activities that seem dangerous to you now even though the activity is, in reality, reasonably safe*. Situations of this type may be specific to your trauma, such as riding in cars (after a car accident). They may also be very general in nature, for example, regardless of the trauma, many people with PTSD avoid crowds, being alone, or both.
2. *Situations that remind you of the traumatic event and you avoid because the memories bring up uncomfortable feelings such as fear, shame, or helplessness.* These include a wide range of trauma reminders such as wearing the same or similar clothing as you wore on the day of the trauma, smelling odors or hearing music that were present during the trauma, and having contact with people who were present during the trauma, even if they were not involved in the trauma. This type of situations can also include simply telling about the details of the trauma.
3. *Situations or activities that are fun or important in your life that you have stopped doing due to loss of interest since the trauma.* This kind of activity can be particularly helpful if you are feeling depressed or withdrawn after experiencing a trauma. These exposures include re-engaging in sports, clubs, hobbies, friendships, family responsibilities such as chores, and other enjoyable or important activities that may have been neglected in the aftermath of the traumatic experience.

Real-life Experiments Step-by-Step

List the situations you have been avoiding, then rate each situation using the stress thermometer. You will re-rate the situations in the last session of the program.

Real-Life Experiments	Initial Rating	Final Rating
Talking to a friend about the accident	5	1
Sitting in the front of a bus	6	2
Wearing my seatbelt	5	0
Sitting in the front seat of the car	7	1
Walking on the sidewalk along a busy street	4	2
Sound of sirens	6	0
Driving/riding over 25–30 mph	9	2
Being inside a hospital, especially the ER area	6	2
Driving or riding in cars at night	10	0
Wearing a turtleneck or neck scarf (feels confining)	7	0
Driving near a large truck or van	10	1
Smell of gasoline	9	1

Figure 6.3 Example of a Completed Hierarchy for a Motor Vehicle Accident Survivor

Real-life Experiments Step-by-Step

List the situations you have been avoiding, then rate each situation using the stress thermometer. You will re-rate the situations in the last session of the program.

Real-Life Experiments	Initial Rating	Final Rating

Staying Safe

It is important that the situations you choose to confront are safe or involve low risk. Do not include dangerous or risky situations on your hierarchy. Instead, work with your therapist to find other ways to confront the fear associated with that situation. For example, if you avoid walking alone at night, plan to walk in a safer area of the city rather than an area known to be a high-crime area.

Instructions for Real-life Experiments

You will begin doing your real-life experiments for the situations on your hierarchy that make you feel somewhat anxious, around a 4 or 5 rating on the stress thermometer. You will progress to more difficult situations in later sessions after you have mastered the easier ones. With some situations you may need to vary the conditions to get your anxiety to go to the chosen level. For example, some situations are less frightening in daytime rather than nighttime, and some situations are more tolerable when you do them with someone rather than alone. Your therapist will help you vary the conditions of the situations on your hierarchy to get just the right level of anxiety for your first real-life experiment. You can also refer to the following example.

Example: Driving on the Highway

In this example, each situation is attempted in turn so that the person is gradually able to return to driving on the highway. The person does not progress to the next situation until his peak anxiety in the previous situation stays lower than about half the original rating for the situation.

Goal: To drive on the highway again

1. You are a passenger in a car driven by your "coach" (supportive friend or family member) around a suburban neighborhood.
2. You drive the car around the suburban neighborhood with your coach as a passenger.
3. You drive on a multilane city street with your coach as a passenger.
4. You are a passenger in a car driven by your coach on the highway during low traffic time.
5. You drive, with your coach as a passenger, on the highway during low traffic time.
6. You drive with your coach as a passenger during moderately heavy traffic time.
7. You drive alone on the highway during moderately heavy traffic time.
8. You drive alone on the highway during heavy traffic time.

When you first practice an experiment, you may feel anxious or frightened. For example, it is possible that your heart will begin racing, your palms will become sweaty, and you will start to tremble. You may want to leave the situation immediately. However, in order for the experiment to succeed and for you to overcome your fears, it is important that you remain in the situation for 30–45 minutes or until the anxiety decreases. After your anxiety decreases by half according to the stress thermometer, you may stop the experiment and move on to different activities.

Remember if you stop the experiment while feeling very anxious, you will not learn that the situation is actually not dangerous. The next time you face the same situation your anxiety level will be very high again. However, if you remain in the situation, your fear and anxiety will decrease. Eventually, you will be able to approach the same situation without feeling fear or anxiety. The more you practice, the less frightened you will feel and the less you will feel the need to avoid the situation.

Keeping Track of Your Progress

Each time you do a real-life experiment, write your stress thermometer rating before and after the experiment on the Real-Life Experiments Data form. The form also includes a place to record your highest stress thermometer rating during the experiment. You and your therapist will go over this form each session to see how you are progressing and to plan the next experiment. See the example of a completed form (Figure 6.4) included in this chapter. You can see in this example how the peak anxiety decreases with practice.

The Dos and Don'ts of Real-Life Experiments

Dos

- *Be gradual*—advance at a gradual pace
- *Be repetitive*—repeat experiments over and over again
- *Be methodical or systematic*—follow the hierarchical list and do not jump from ranking to ranking
- *Be reflective*—predict what will happen and test the results
- *Be effortful*—invest in practicing experiments that may not be part of your daily routine

Don'ts

- *Don't compare yourself to others*—compare yourself only to yourself, and advance at your own pace
- *Don't be impulsive*—think before you act
- *Don't avoid or escape*—do not stop the experiment early or avoid the situation in any way

Real-life Experiments Data

Record your stress ratings before and after each real-life experiment. Also record the highest stress rating that you experienced during the real-life experiment.

REMINDER: Remain in the situation for at least 30–45 minutes or until the stress ratings have decreased by half.

Situation: riding as a passenger in a car (to school, mom driving)

Date & Time	Before	After	Highest
4/17/05	8	8	9
4/19/05	8	6	8
4/21/05	6	5	6
4/22/05	4	3	4
4/23/05	3	3	3

Situation: sitting with friends at lunch

Date & Time	Before	After	Highest
4/17/05	10	4	10
4/18/05	6	3	6
4/19/05	4	3	5
4/20/05	2	2	2
4/21/05	2	2	2
4/22/05	2	1	2

Figure 6.4 Example of a Completed Form for a Motor Vehicle Accident Survivor

Homework

- ✎ Review this chapter for homework.
- ✎ Listen to the recording of the session.
- ✎ Start real-life experiments using the stress thermometer and record your ratings on the Real-Life Experiments Data form.
- ✎ Add avoidance situations as necessary to the Real-Life Experiments Step-by-Step form.
- ✎ Continue practicing relaxed breathing exercise.

Real-life Experiments Data

Record your stress ratings before and after each real-life experiment. Also record the highest stress rating that you experienced during the real-life experiment.

REMINDER: Remain in the situation for at least 30–45 minutes or until the stress ratings have decreased by half.

Situation:____

Date & Time	Before	After	Highest

Situation:____

Date & Time	Before	After	Highest

Goals

- To understand why it is important to recount the memory of the trauma
- To recount the trauma
- To process the traumatic memory
- To identify unhelpful thoughts and beliefs

Overview

You've already begun to face situations that you avoid because of your fear and anxiety. In this unit, you will also start to confront the memory of the traumatic experience. By recounting the memory again and again, you will learn that the memory itself cannot hurt you. Your therapist will help you process your thoughts and feelings about the traumatic memory so you can move on with your life.

Rationale for Recounting the Memory

After a trauma, many people try to avoid thinking about it. This is because remembering the trauma causes anxiety or other bad feelings such as sadness or anger. You may also be trying to keep memories of the scary incident away to avoid the pain they cause. You may be saying to yourself things like "don't think about it," "time will cure everything," or "I just need to forget about it." It is possible that your friends and family are also telling you to leave the past behind and move on. But the more you make an effort to forget the memories, the more you continue to be bothered by the scary thoughts and feelings. The trauma is actually far from being over for you.

The purpose of therapy in general, and recounting the traumatic memory in particular, is to help you stop being afraid of or upset by the memories related to the trauma. The process is similar to what you experienced in real-life experiments. With the help of your therapist, you will confront anxiety-provoking memories that you would otherwise avoid. In order for this to work properly, you must repeat the process again and again, adding in details, thoughts, and feelings as you recall them. As with the real-life experiments, you may feel that your anxiety increases when you first recount the memory. It is only natural to feel distress at first when you recount the memory of a traumatic event. But the more you face the memory of the trauma—instead of avoiding it—the more you will see that the memory itself cannot harm you and that your anxiety gradually decreases with time.

You can think of the traumatic experience as being kept in your memory like a book. You are trying to keep this book closed and never read it. But, what is actually happening is that the book opens by itself, suddenly and unexpectedly, on different pages, and you find yourself "reading" scary parts against your will. The goal is for you to read this book from beginning to end several times until some order is put into the pages. As a result, in the future, you will be able to open up the book on whatever page you want, read it, browse through it, or just leave it closed, not out of fear but out of boredom.

It may still seem that the best plan would be to simply put the memory out of your mind. Unfortunately, this plan does not work for most people. Try to recall if you have ever been able to simply put the memory out of your mind and have it *stay* out of your mind. Even though it seems like a simple task, it is likely that the memory crept back in and continued to bother you even though you may have tried very hard to push it away. In fact, most people find that when they try to push a thought away, it actually comes back to bother them more often than ever before.

Thought-Stopping Experiment

Here is an experiment to help you understand how difficult it is to stop your thoughts. You may do this experiment, or one like it, with your therapist during a session, but it works just as well to try it on your own.

> *Get comfortable. Start thinking about whatever comes into your mind. You can think of anything you wish, except, whatever you do, DO NOT think about a small purple elephant. You can think of anything else, any kind of animal, or any thought at all, but DO NOT think of a small purple elephant. If a thought or a picture of a small purple elephant pops into your mind, push it out as best you can. Give yourself 2–3 minutes to let the thought of the small purple elephant leave your mind.*

Now be very honest with yourself and review what was going through your mind while you were pushing away the thought of the small purple elephant. Did you get images of the elephant? Did the thought of it creep in every time you chased it away? Most people find it very difficult to have the thought stay away for more than a minute or two. Perhaps you were successful in avoiding the thought for a short time. How much effort did this require? Some people find they are able to chase the thought away for a time, but the effort is so great it interferes with their ability to do everyday activities.

Trying to push away a scary memory is just like trying to push away that thought of the small purple elephant. The harder you work to push away the memory, the more it seems to bother you. Even if you are successful in pushing it away for awhile, the effort is so great it becomes very difficult to focus on other, more important things.

Effects of Recounting the Memory

Recounting the traumatic memory helps you recover from trauma-related problems in several ways. These are described as follows.

Digesting the Memories

Some people like to think of processing the memory as "digestion." Suppose you have eaten a very large meal that you cannot digest. This feels very uncomfortable doesn't it? Your stomach rumbles and it may even hurt. The way to feel better is to digest the food. Likewise, your scary feelings, bad dreams, and upsetting thoughts are happening because they have not been digested well by your mind. Since you can't be rid of the experience or the memory once a trauma has happened, much like a bad meal, you simply have to digest it in order to feel better. By recounting and processing your trauma memories, you can start to digest them so they will stop interfering with your life.

Discriminating Between the Trauma and the Memory

Being exposed to the memory will enable you to discriminate between the trauma itself and the memory of the trauma. That is, it will help you realize that the trauma happened in the past, and that now is not the past, even if you think about the trauma. During the trauma, there was real danger and a reason to be anxious and scared. But the memory of the trauma is not dangerous; there is no need to be scared or anxious while remembering the trauma. By recounting the trauma, you will learn that the memory does not have any power over you; it is only a memory.

Organizing the Memory

Telling the story over and over again helps organize the memory. A traumatic memory is often jumbled and confusing. Some parts seem to play over and over again in your mind while other parts are forgotten or mixed up. This can make you feel frightened and off balance. By staying with the memories, you will begin to make sense of the trauma so that it won't feel so confusing and dangerous. You will begin to learn things as you do this. One of the things you can learn very quickly is that remembering and telling the story of the trauma does not harm you.

Getting Used to the Memories (Habituation)

Continuous recounting of the trauma will reduce your anxiety. It will teach you that anxiety does not last forever and that you do not need to run away from the memory in order to stop your fear and anxiety. The more you recall and recount the trauma, the better this process will work. Repetition is necessary to get used to the memories and decrease anxiety.

Gaining Control

You may feel that the anxiety of recalling the trauma will make you "fall to pieces" or go crazy. The fear of losing control is understandable and natural, but you will not fall to pieces and you will not go crazy. In fact, the more you practice recounting the memory, the more your sense of control will increase. You will discover that you have the power to overcome anxiety, as well as other obstacles in your life.

Recounting the Memory of the Trauma

Before you begin to recount the memory, your therapist will help you decide where to begin and end the story. When you are ready to begin, your therapist will ask you for a stress thermometer rating before starting. Next, you will close your eyes and tell the story, as it happened, from the beginning to the end. You will tell the story in the present time, as if it is happening now, for example, "I am walking/driving/sitting/etc." Your story should be as detailed as you can remember. You will talk about what happened, and what you were thinking and feeling at the time. You will mention all the things that happened to you. You should include everything you remember. Don't worry about doing it perfectly, especially the first time. If you forget, your therapist may help you by reminding you to keep your eyes closed or to stay in the present tense. As you tell the story, your therapist will ask, every few minutes, for a stress thermometer rating. You will answer by saying the number that best matches your level of anxiety at that moment. Once you finish recounting the story, you will keep your eyes closed. If you have time left in session, your therapist will say "from the beginning." You will again start recounting the story from the beginning. As you get more experience telling the memory, your therapist may ask you to add details about what you are feeling and thinking as the story goes on. This will help you get in touch with all the parts of the memory in order to digest the entire experience.

Processing the Memory of the Trauma

When recounting the memory is over, your therapist will help you process the memory of the trauma by discussing your feelings about it and by helping you think about the memory in different ways. Together you will compare your stress thermometer ratings at the beginning and at the end of the exposure. You may notice that your scared and sad feelings get less upsetting as you keep working on the memory. This is great because it will help you see how helpful recounting of the trauma can be. But don't worry if this doesn't happen the first time around. Some people find that they need several sessions before they see real reduction in their anxiety.

Identifying Unhelpful Thoughts and Beliefs

Much of your current distress may come from the way you think about the trauma now, rather than from the particular thoughts that went through your mind at the time of the event itself. These unhelpful or unrealistic thoughts and beliefs fuel negative emotions, like guilt, shame, and anger and strengthen your other PTSD symptoms. In processing the memory, your therapist will help you identify and examine the unhelpful thoughts and beliefs that are at the root of your current distress. The goal is to increase your awareness of these thoughts and beliefs and to change them when needed.

When you become aware of unhelpful thoughts and beliefs, it is useful to challenge them with the following questions:

- What is the "hard" evidence for this thought?
- Is the thought accurate or is it exaggerated?
- What would you tell a good friend if he said to you that he felt the way you describe?
- Can you think of a different way of looking at the situation?

Challenging your thoughts in this way can help you find more helpful and realistic ways of viewing your difficult experiences and can help to reduce the distress you feel when you think about the trauma.

Working With the Memory at Home

After each session of recounting the memory, your therapist will give you a recording of the memory to listen to at home once per day. This is an important part of the treatment because it allows you to confront the memory many more times than you would be able to do if you only told the story in session. When you listen at home, you will rate your stress at the beginning and end and identify when your stress was highest just as you did in the real-life experiments. You can keep track of the ratings on the Recounting the Memory Data form.

Making Progress

In the next few sessions, you will continue to recount the memory as you did the first time. Your therapist will continue to help you identify thoughts, feelings, and details so that the memory becomes much more organized and complete. You and your therapist may even change where you start and stop the story to help you focus on the most important thoughts and feelings. After a session or two, you will have more experience telling the story and you will hopefully begin to notice your stress ratings are getting less intense. If not, your therapist will work with you to adjust the way you are recounting the memory to help you reduce your anxiety.

Homework

✎ Review this chapter for homework.
✎ Listen to the recording of the session.
✎ Listen to the recording of recounting the memory daily and write down your level of distress on the Recounting the Memory Data form. (Copies

of the form can be found at the end of the book. You may photocopy this form as needed.)

✎ Choose real-life experiments from your hierarchy to practice for homework. Track stress thermometer ratings on the Real-Life Experiments Data form. (Copies of the form can be found at the end of the book. You may photocopy this form as needed.)

Recounting the Memory Data

Record your stress ratings before and after each time you recount the memory. Also record the highest stress rating that you experienced during recounting the memory.

Date & Time	Before	After	Highest

Notes:

Chapter 8: Worst Moments

Goals

- To recount the most difficult parts of the trauma
- To process and digest the most difficult parts of the trauma

Overview

As recounting the memory of the trauma becomes easier, you will begin to concentrate on the parts of the trauma that are most distressing to you. Instead of recounting the memory of the entire trauma from beginning to end, you will focus only on the hard parts or the "worst moments" of the trauma memory. Your therapist will help you process your thoughts and feelings about each of these moments.

Recounting Worst Moments

You and your therapist together will identify the "worst moments" of your trauma memory. You will be recounting each of these moments one at a time. You will pick one to begin with, and will work on the others later. In session, you will focus in on each memory as if you are zooming in for a close-up. You will recount what happened with as much detail as possible. This includes what you felt, saw, heard, and thought in that part of the memory. You will work on that part until you feel that you have "worn it out" and your stress thermometer rating has decreased. When that part is done, you will move on to the next one.

You will review the worst moments one at a time in a repetitive manner (as many as 6–7 times) during a single session. Just as you did when recounting the entire trauma memory, you will close your eyes and recall the moment in the present tense. You will give as many details as possible about your thoughts, feelings, and sensations during these exposures. Your therapist will ask for stress thermometer ratings every few minutes. When your stress ratings decrease to a range of 2 or 3, the exposure will end. Your therapist will then help you to begin processing the emotions and thoughts associated with that section of the story.

Processing the Memory of the Trauma

As you did when processing the entire trauma memory, you and your therapist will discuss your thoughts and feelings associated with the worst moments. You will also review the stress ratings associated with each worst moment. For homework, you will listen to recordings of your worst moments and keep track of your stress ratings as before. When the stress ratings associated with each worst moment are reduced to 3 or less, this unit is finished.

Looking Forward

As you come to the end of this part of your treatment, you and your therapist will begin thinking about and discussing what happened during your treatment and what things will be like after treatment is complete. This will include thinking about what you have learned about your trauma, how your symptoms have changed, and what skills you will take with you as you finish treatment. You will also begin thinking about the future and identifying possible challenges that might come up. Before you finish treatment, you and your therapist will identify possible experiences that could cause you to have a temporary increase in symptoms. Then you will review what you have learned to create a plan to cope with these "triggers."

Homework

- ✎ Review this chapter for homework.
- ✎ Listen to the recording of the session.
- ✎ Listen to the recording of recounting worst moments at least once a day. Track stress thermometer ratings on the Recounting Worst Moments form. (Copies of the form can be found at the end of the book. You may photocopy this form as needed.)
- ✎ Choose real-life experiments from your hierarchy to practice for homework. Track stress thermometer ratings on the Real-Life Experiments Data form. (Copies of the form can be found at the end of the book. You may photocopy this form as needed.)
- ✎ After the last session of this unit, complete the Triggers and Tools form to prepare for the next unit.

Recounting Worst Moments Data

Record your stress ratings before and after each time you recount a worst moment. Also record the highest stress rating that you experienced during recounting the worst moment.

Worst Moment:______________________________

Date & Time	Before	After	Highest

Worst Moment:______________________________

Date & Time	Before	After	Highest

Triggers and Tools

Situations which may cause stress in the future	Ways to cope with stressful situations

Goals

- To identify potential symptom triggers
- To plan coping strategies for symptom relapse
- To review tools acquired in therapy

Overview

The bulk of this unit will be spent reviewing the Triggers and Tools form completed as homework in the previous session. You and your therapist will discuss how you can cope with future challenges using the tools you have learned in therapy. You will also make preparations for finishing therapy.

Identification of Triggers

Your therapy will soon be coming to an end, and many of your anxieties and difficulties have decreased. It is now time to think about what may cause distress or aggravate your symptoms in the future. You have already begun to do this by preparing the Triggers and Tools form for homework. You and your therapist will review your list of triggers and makes sure it includes all areas of your life. Following are common life areas and examples of potential triggers.

Trauma-Related Events: reminders and unfinished business related to the trauma, such as anniversary dates, memorial services, or appearing in court.

Additional Traumatic Events: coping with an additional traumatic event that happens to you or to someone close to you.

Health Problems: coping with additional health problems.

School: starting at a new school; studying for and taking exams; going on school trips that include sleeping away from home; dealing with the requirements of strict teachers; receiving bad grades; accepting criticism.

Social life: changes in your social circle; problems with friends; dating someone new; coping with a breakup.

Family Life: death of a relative; divorce; changes in family dynamics (birth of a sibling, sibling leaving home, etc.).

Any new ideas should be added to your Triggers and Tools form. An additional blank form is included in this chapter. You may photocopy this form as needed.

Triggers and Tools

Situations which may cause stress in the future	Ways to cope with stressful situations

Planning Coping Strategies

Next you and your therapist will discuss how to cope with these triggers and overcome them. Your coping strategies will be listed next to the corresponding situations on the Triggers and Tools form. Remember, you can use strategies you learned in therapy in future situations. You can ask yourself "What did we do in therapy when I encountered a similar problem?" Do not forget to use additional sources of help within your family, community, school, etc. For example, if you encounter a new and frightening situation, you may wish to discuss the situation with a parent or friend. They can help you to determine if the situation is really dangerous or simply triggering unhelpful or unrealistic thoughts. If the situation is not dangerous, you will know from therapy that it is best to confront this kind of fear. You can then design graduated exposures to help yourself overcome the fear.

Review of Tools

During therapy, you have acquired several strategies and skills (see following descriptions). You and your therapist will review these and discuss how you might apply each one in the future.

Real-life Experiments

By practicing real-life experiments repeatedly you overcame your avoidance. You had a chance to learn the facts about a situation. You got used to doing things that seemed scary or uncomfortable beforehand. You were also able to start doing things that you had stopped doing since the trauma. As a result, you felt better about yourself.

Recounting the Memory

When you faced your fearful thoughts they became less powerful. Once you stopped avoiding the memories that made you feel scared, you began to feel stronger and more in control of your thoughts.

Challenging Thoughts

You learned how to question your beliefs about yourself, others, and the world. You challenged your thinking to make sure it was in line with reality. You became very skilled at recognizing when you were letting the trauma or other unpleasant situations distort how you were thinking about the present. Once you were able to recognize unhelpful and unrealistic thoughts, you could change them to be more useful.

Pleasurable Activities

Engaging in pleasurable activities even when your mood was down made you feel better. As a result of doing things you enjoyed, your mood actually improved. You learned that you should not wait for your mood to pick up in order to take part in pleasurable activities.

Sharing Emotions

Talking about your feelings with trusted family and friends gave you a sense of relief and helped you to feel more connected to others in your life. It also assisted in digesting your feelings.

Breathing

As you have learned, the way we breathe can affect how we feel. Practicing slow, calm breathing helped you to slow down and feel more relaxed.

Summary

You now own all these tools and can keep using them after therapy ends. Just like riding a bicycle, once you learn how, you never forget, even if you have not ridden for a long time. You will be able to keep all these tricks and tools and use them whenever you need to. The next time you find yourself in a challenging situation, remember that you have faced difficult tasks that seemed impossible at first.

Final Project

Some people like to have something they can take with them that summarizes or celebrates the hard work they have done. This "final project" is most often a written work, but if you like to draw or do other kinds of activities that are meaningful to you, you might find a way to use those skills and talents as well. Here are some ideas that you might include:

1. *Cover Sheet*—name the book that you "wrote" about your scary memory and either draw or print out a picture that has meaning to you.
2. *What Happened to Me*—write or type out the entire memory narrative.
3. *After the Trauma*—write about things that changed for you after the trauma, including your PTSD symptoms, your feelings and beliefs, family changes, etc. Be sure to include a paragraph or more about how you feel now in comparison, in order to make this activity a positive one.
4. *What I Learned in Therapy*—write about the major techniques learned (breathing exercise, real-life experiments, and recounting the memory) as well as why they were used and how you may be able to use them in the future.
5. *A Letter to the Perpetrator*—write a letter (not meant to be sent) to the perpetrator (if there is one in your trauma) about how you feel now about what happened.

6. *Ten Years From Now*—write in detail about what you want to be doing in 10 years.
7. *Ten Good Things About Me*—write ten things about yourself that are positive.
8. *Taking Care of Myself*—identify things that upset you and problem solve ways to address these issues in the future
9. *Three Wishes for Myself and the World (And How I Can Make Them Come True)*—identify three wishes as well as make a plan for how you can accomplish them.

If you want to do a final project, talk it over with your therapist, who may have additional good ideas or suggestions on what to include.

You may also wish to share your accomplishments with your parents or other significant people in your life by sharing your final project with them or by inviting them to attend part of your last session to celebrate the end of treatment. If you wish to include anyone in your last session, be sure to discuss it with your therapist. Also remember to invite the people you want to attend ahead of time.

Homework

- ✎ Review this chapter for homework.
- ✎ Listen to the recording of the session.
- ✎ Complete any projects or plans needed for the final session.
- ✎ Continue with any real-life experiments left on your hierarchy. Track stress thermometer ratings on the Real-Life Experiments Data form. (Copies of the form can be found at the end of the book.)

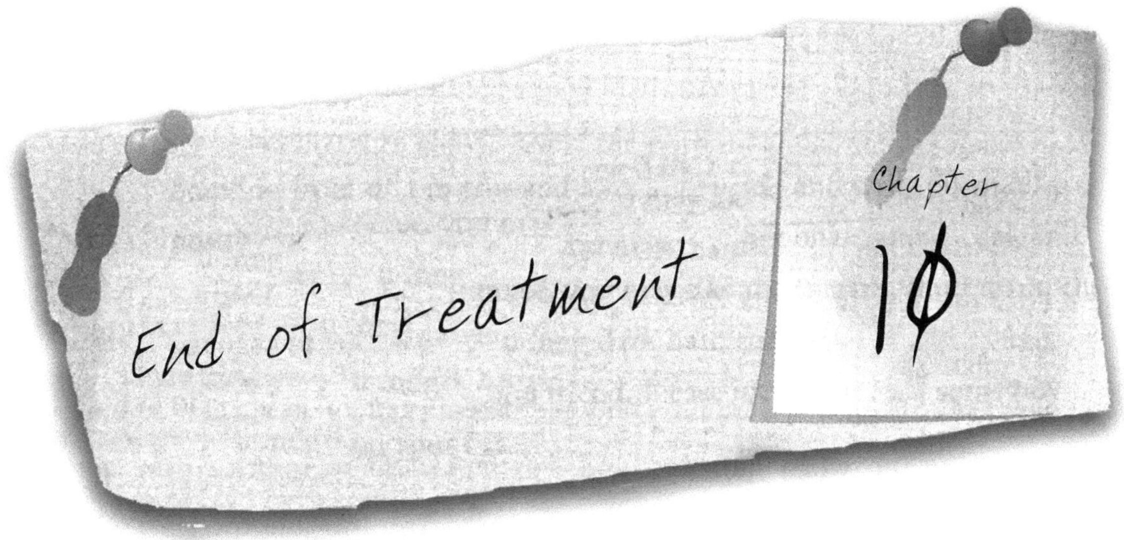

Goals

- To recount the memory
- To review your progress and identify any remaining areas that need work
- To wrap up treatment and celebrate your accomplishments

Overview

This is the final unit. Part of the session will be spent recounting the memory and discussing your feelings about it. You will spend the rest of the session wrapping up, that is, discussing what has been helpful, what has not been so helpful, how things have changed for you, and what is left to work on after treatment ends. You will also talk about how you can use the skills you learned in treatment to help you in the future, whether you face new challenges, or whether some old feelings and concerns pop up to bother you. Finally, since this is the end of treatment, you and your therapist will spend some time discussing any feelings you have about going forward on your own.

The last session is also a time to recognize and celebrate all your hard work. You may decide to use part of the session to share your accomplishments with others, or simply to acknowledge them with your therapist alone. Either way, you deserve to celebrate!

Recounting the Memory for the Last Time

You will spend part of the session recounting the entire memory again. You have completed work on the worst moments and it is important to return to the complete memory to see how you feel about this memory now. You and your therapist will spend some time processing the memory as you have done in the other sessions, but this time, you will focus on how the experience of telling the memory has changed for you since the beginning of treatment. How have your stress thermometer ratings changed since the first time you recounted the memory? Have your feelings changed? Has the memory itself changed in any way? Do you view the trauma differently than before treatment? Do you feel differently about yourself?

Reviewing Your Progress

You have spent many weeks facing your fears using the techniques you learned in the treatment. You have been reviewing your progress every session by comparing your anxiety ratings from week to week, and discussing changes in your symptoms with your therapist. Hopefully, you have been noticing changes in your activities and your level of enjoyment in life as well. In this session, you and your therapist will go back to the very first session and review your progress from the beginning. You may discover some changes that were not easy to notice in your week-to-week discussions. You may also notice areas that still need improvement. How are you feeling about these changes? What do they mean for your future? Are there things you still need to learn? As you are taking stock, think about what was helpful or not helpful to you in the treatment (recounting the memory in session, breathing, processing, listening to tapes at home, etc.).

You and your therapist will use the hierarchy of real-life experiments that you created in that unit to help with reviewing your progress. As your therapist reads the activities on the list, try to imagine you are doing each activity right now. Your therapist will ask you for a stress thermometer rating for each activity. After you have rated all the activities on the list, you will compare your final stress thermometer ratings to your ratings at the beginning of treatment to see how your level of stress has changed. You may be pleasantly surprised to find out how much you have improved. Most people find that their anxiety level has decreased a lot. What does this mean in real life? Is it easier to do the things you want and need to do? How did it happen? What did you learn about yourself and your ability to face your fear?

Look more closely at the list of activities. Did some items decrease more than others? Think about why that might be. Many people find that the items they practiced a lot come down a great deal. The items they practiced very little remain high. Are you still avoiding some things on the list? Were there activities that you did not get to because you ran out of time? Just because treatment is ending does not mean you should stop doing the real-life experiments. In fact, just the opposite is true. Continue doing real-life experiments with those remaining items on the list. Your therapist can help you come up with a plan to address the remaining items. You may want to use the extra copy of the Real-Life Experiments Step-by-Step form at the end of this chapter. You may photocopy this form as needed.

Continuing to practice the real-life experiments and the other skills you have learned in the treatment has other benefits as well. Many people feel better at the end of treatment, but they also worry that they could easily fall back into old habits of avoidance and unhelpful thinking. This makes a lot of sense if you think of it like an exercise program. How many people have struggled to get into shape only to fall back into old patterns soon after they reached their goal? Practice will keep you from returning to your old ways. Regular practice can also help you feel even better than you do now. Research with this treatment has shown that most people feel better at the end of treatment, but many of those same people will feel even better 6 months later even though they didn't receive any more treatment. We think this happens because they changed the way they cope with daily stresses. That is, they went from avoiding scary, unfamiliar, or challenging experiences to facing those experiences and getting past them.

Your therapist will ask you for feedback about the overall therapy experience, too. Your feedback is an important way to make sure that treatments, such as the one you have just finished, continue to improve. Let your therapist know about all the helpful things you experienced in the treatment. If something was not so helpful, or if you think the treatment could be improved in a particular way, be sure to let your therapist know about that as well.

Feelings About Ending Treatment

You may feel relief or even excitement that treatment is finally over. But it is also normal to feel sad or afraid of "going it alone." These are all natural feelings that come up sometimes as a person faces the end of treatment. You shared some very personal and painful experiences with your therapist, and that required a tremendous amount of trust on your part. For many people who had experienced a traumatic event, trusting the therapist is one of the most difficult steps in the treatment. Now that your therapy relationship is coming to a close, it is normal to wonder if you will be able to find other people with whom you can share your experiences. Be sure to face these feelings just as you have faced the other difficult feelings along the way. Your therapist can help you with this too. Whether you feel relief, sadness, or something else, it is important that you share these feelings about ending therapy with your therapist. Take the time you need to say good-bye. Recognize the risk you took in trusting your therapist and sharing the intimate details of your life. Honor the struggle you face in leaving treatment, if there is a struggle. If instead, you feel relief and excitement, honor those feelings too. One of the lessons of this treatment is that whatever you feel, it is important to allow those feelings to have a place in your life—to face them, process them, and recognize that you can cope with them.

End of Therapy

Congratulations on completing the program! You have just completed an intense and very personal treatment. You should be congratulated for the effort and time you have invested in conquering your PTSD symptoms. You may feel that you are completely recovered or you may feel that you still need to work on some areas in order to feel completely free of your symptoms. Regardless of where you are at, we hope that you continue to use the techniques you learned in treatment. Remember, you can use these skills to face any difficult experiences or emotions that come up for you in the future.

You worked very hard to learn new skills for facing your fears. These new skills are yours to keep. But more than just a set of skills, we hope you learned a new way of thinking about your fear and anxiety. Hopefully, you will never experience another traumatic event, but you will almost certainly have some experiences that challenge you, even frighten you, because they are new, unfamiliar, or unpleasant. When you meet these new challenges, you will have a helpful way of thinking about these experiences and skills to help you manage your feelings.

The main lesson we hope you have learned is that facing your fears can help you overcome them. Avoidance, on the other hand, will keep you stuck in your fear and rob you of your freedom to live your life the way you wish. This is as true for everyday fears and anxieties as it is for trauma-related fear and anxiety.

We hope you are proud of your accomplishments and that you will continue to use what you have learned to meet life's challenges and live the life you want.

Real-life Experiments Step-by-Step

List the situations you have been avoiding, then rate each situation using the stress thermometer. You will re-rate the situations in the last session of the program.

Real-Life Experiments	**Initial Rating**	**Final Rating**

Real-life Experiments Data

Record your stress ratings before and after each real-life experiment. Also record the highest stress rating that you experienced during the real-life experiment.

REMINDER: Remain in the situation for at least 30–45 minutes or until the stress ratings have decreased by half.

Situation:____

Date & Time	Before	After	Highest

Situation:____

Date & Time	Before	After	Highest

Real-life Experiments Data

Record your stress ratings before and after each real-life experiment. Also record the highest stress rating that you experienced during the real-life experiment.

REMINDER: Remain in the situation for at least 30–45 minutes or until the stress ratings have decreased by half.

Situation:____

Date & Time	**Before**	**After**	**Highest**

Situation:____

Date & Time	**Before**	**After**	**Highest**

Real-life Experiments Data

Record your stress ratings before and after each real-life experiment. Also record the highest stress rating that you experienced during the real-life experiment.

REMINDER: Remain in the situation for at least 30–45 minutes or until the stress ratings have decreased by half.

Situation:____

Date & Time	Before	After	Highest

Situation:____

Date & Time	Before	After	Highest

Real-life Experiments Data

Record your stress ratings before and after each real-life experiment. Also record the highest stress rating that you experienced during the real-life experiment.

REMINDER: Remain in the situation for at least 30–45 minutes or until the stress ratings have decreased by half.

Situation:____

Date & Time	Before	After	Highest

Situation:____

Date & Time	Before	After	Highest

Real-life Experiments Data

Record your stress ratings before and after each real-life experiment. Also record the highest stress rating that you experienced during the real-life experiment.

REMINDER: Remain in the situation for at least 30–45 minutes or until the stress ratings have decreased by half.

Situation:______________________________________

Date & Time	Before	After	Highest

Situation:______________________________________

Date & Time	Before	After	Highest

Real-life Experiments Data

Record your stress ratings before and after each real-life experiment. Also record the highest stress rating that you experienced during the real-life experiment.

REMINDER: Remain in the situation for at least 30–45 minutes or until the stress ratings have decreased by half.

Situation:______________________________________

Date & Time	Before	After	Highest

Situation:______________________________________

Date & Time	Before	After	Highest

Real-life Experiments Data

Record your stress ratings before and after each real-life experiment. Also record the highest stress rating that you experienced during the real-life experiment.

REMINDER: Remain in the situation for at least 30–45 minutes or until the stress ratings have decreased by half.

Situation:____

Date & Time	**Before**	**After**	**Highest**

Situation:____

Date & Time	**Before**	**After**	**Highest**

Real-life Experiments Data

Record your stress ratings before and after each real-life experiment. Also record the highest stress rating that you experienced during the real-life experiment.

REMINDER: Remain in the situation for at least 30–45 minutes or until the stress ratings have decreased by half.

Situation: ______________________________

Date & Time	Before	After	Highest
______________	______	______	______
______________	______	______	______
______________	______	______	______
______________	______	______	______
______________	______	______	______
______________	______	______	______
______________	______	______	______

Situation: ______________________________

Date & Time	Before	After	Highest
______________	______	______	______
______________	______	______	______
______________	______	______	______
______________	______	______	______
______________	______	______	______
______________	______	______	______
______________	______	______	______

Recounting the Memory Data

Record your stress ratings before and after each time you recount the memory. Also record the highest stress rating that you experienced during recounting the memory.

Date & Time	**Before**	**After**	**Highest**

Notes:

Recounting the Memory Data

Record your stress ratings before and after each time you recount the memory. Also record the highest stress rating that you experienced during recounting the memory.

Date & Time	Before	After	Highest

Notes:

Recounting the Memory Data

Record your stress ratings before and after each time you recount the memory. Also record the highest stress rating that you experienced during recounting the memory.

Date & Time	Before	After	Highest

Notes:

Recounting the Memory Data

Record your stress ratings before and after each time you recount the memory. Also record the highest stress rating that you experienced during recounting the memory.

Date & Time	Before	After	Highest

Notes:

Recounting the Memory Data

Record your stress ratings before and after each time you recount the memory. Also record the highest stress rating that you experienced during recounting the memory.

Date & Time	**Before**	**After**	**Highest**

Notes:

Recounting the Memory Data

Record your stress ratings before and after each time you recount the memory. Also record the highest stress rating that you experienced during recounting the memory.

Date & Time	Before	After	Highest

Notes:

Recounting the Memory Data

Record your stress ratings before and after each time you recount the memory. Also record the highest stress rating that you experienced during recounting the memory.

Date & Time	**Before**	**After**	**Highest**

Notes:

Recounting the Memory Data

Record your stress ratings before and after each time you recount the memory. Also record the highest stress rating that you experienced during recounting the memory.

Date & Time	**Before**	**After**	**Highest**

Notes:

Recounting Worst Moments Data

Record your stress ratings before and after each time you recount a worst moment. Also record the highest stress rating that you experienced during recounting the worst moment.

Worst Moment:_______________________________

Date & Time	**Before**	**After**	**Highest**

Worst Moment:_______________________________

Date & Time	**Before**	**After**	**Highest**

Recounting Worst Moments Data

Record your stress ratings before and after each time you recount a worst moment. Also record the highest stress rating that you experienced during recounting the worst moment.

Worst Moment:________________________________

Date & Time	Before	After	Highest

Worst Moment:________________________________

Date & Time	Before	After	Highest

Recounting Worst Moments Data

Record your stress ratings before and after each time you recount a worst moment. Also record the highest stress rating that you experienced during recounting the worst moment.

Worst Moment: ______________________________

Date & Time	Before	After	Highest

Worst Moment: ______________________________

Date & Time	Before	After	Highest

Recounting Worst Moments Data

Record your stress ratings before and after each time you recount a worst moment. Also record the highest stress rating that you experienced during recounting the worst moment.

Worst Moment:____

Date & Time	Before	After	Highest

Worst Moment:____

Date & Time	Before	After	Highest

Recounting Worst Moments Data

Record your stress ratings before and after each time you recount a worst moment. Also record the highest stress rating that you experienced during recounting the worst moment.

Worst Moment:____

Date & Time	**Before**	**After**	**Highest**

Worst Moment:____

Date & Time	**Before**	**After**	**Highest**

Recounting Worst Moments Data

Record your stress ratings before and after each time you recount a worst moment. Also record the highest stress rating that you experienced during recounting the worst moment.

Worst Moment:____________________________________

Date & Time	Before	After	Highest

Worst Moment:____________________________________

Date & Time	Before	After	Highest

Printed in the USA/Agawam, MA
November 10, 2020

764185.140

TABLE OF CONTENTS

THRIVE IN LIFE

From start to finish, these 7 Core Truths are intended to be built on top of one another, leading you from where you are now to a more profound faith, love, hope, and purpose in life.

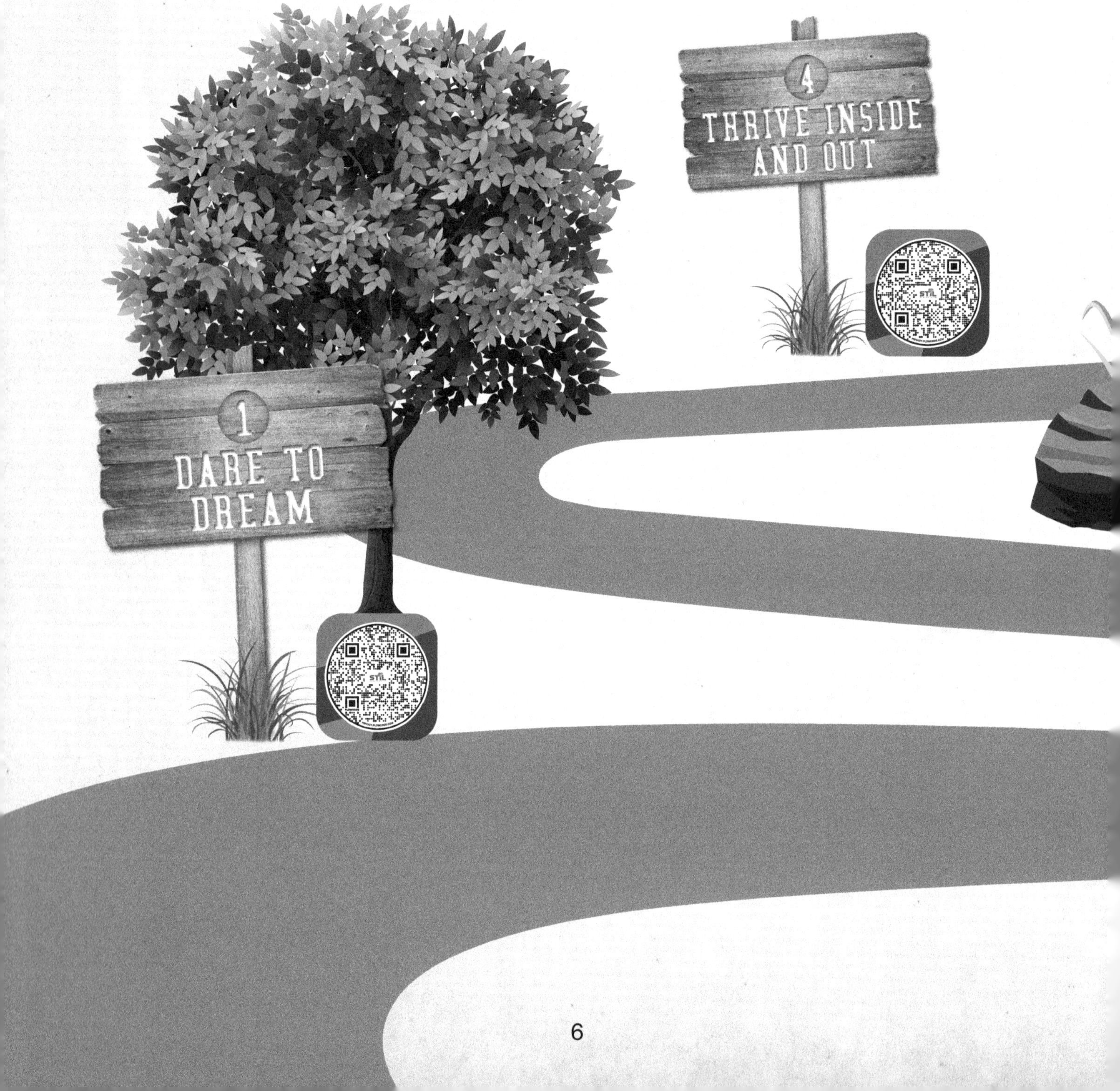

4
THRIVE INSIDE AND OUT

1
DARE TO DREAM

"Your word is a lamp to guide my feet
and a light for my path."
Psalm 119:105

Core Truth 1:
DARE TO DREAM

**"'For I know the plans I have for you' says the Lord,
'They are plans for good and not for disaster,
to give you a future and hope.'"**
Jeremiah 29:11

WELCOME
to
DARE TO DREAM

The purpose of Dare to Dream is to help you create or confirm fresh purpose, plans, and vision in your life.

Scan the code with your mobile device for a video introducing Dare To Dream.

THE MAP: GOD'S WORD

God says in His Word that He has created you with a purpose, filled you with good plans, and given you a hope and future *(Jeremiah 29:11)*. He selected you to bear good fruit *(John 15:16)*, which means positive outward actions because of the change God created inwardly in your heart. God desires for you to determine and write down the vision/dream He gave you in your heart and pursue it until it is completed *(Habakkuk 2:2-3, Hebrews 12:1)*.

It is important to dream. A dream can be two things. It can be an inspiring picture or revelation from God *(Joel 2:28)*. A dream can also be a personal picture in your imagination that inspires possibilities for the future. Dreaming allows you to stay hopeful during difficult times but also reignites passion, which needs rekindling sometimes. God has designed you with the ability to dream so your hope will never desert you. Your God is a kind God. And when you commit your life to Him, He provides you with all you need. Each morning when you begin your day, dare yourself to achieve divinely inspired dreams/visions.

PRACTICAL STEPS FOR YOUR JOURNEY

THOUGHTS FOR THE JOURNEY:

Everyone, at every age and stage, can dream. It is okay to not have a clear vision/dream today.

Take a moment to reflect on where you are right now and with previously realized dreams.

Seeking perfection, procrastinating, or holding on to past disappointments and hurts, will slow your progress toward your dream. Life is meant to be lived in the present not in the past or future.

Mistakes, missteps, and even failures are part of the journey and can help grow your dream.

Faith is believing and trusting in God with hope and expectation. It does not ignore facts or reality, but it embraces that God and His Word are greater than anything you are experiencing.

ACTIONS FOR THE JOURNEY:

- Pause. Set aside some uninterrupted quiet time to use your imagination while inviting, including, and talking with God about your dream.
- Practice listening and being still before God to hear Him speak.
- Take a deep breath, go slow, and take manageable steps.
- Recognize there will be gaps while you are developing your dream; look for them, and work to find answers.
- Keep an eye out for negative habits, routines, and roles that are holding you back from achieving your dream/vision, and replace them with more beneficial ones.
- Find people to share your dream with who will be there to support you as you make it a reality.
- If you have forgotten how to dream, give yourself permission to be playful and creative.

- Embrace the grace (God's riches at Christ's expense) of God, which is His free gift to you, through Jesus Christ. You can not earn it. You don't deserve it. It is the favor and approval of God *(Ephesians 2:8-9)*.

ROADBLOCKS COMMON IN THE JOURNEY:

Past disappointments
Procrastination
Fear
Apathy
Comfort with status quo
Discouragement or sadness
Lacking self-confidence
Overwhelmed or stressed

Unhelpful thinking
Jealousy or envy
Pride
Selfishness
Self-sabotage
False guilt
Shame
Anger

Bitterness or resentment
Certain realities:
limited time and money
Life circumstances:
single, parent, widowed, divorced, physical health, change in personal life, mental health

When you identify a roadblock, call on God to help you overcome that roadblock and choose a new path. Know that Jesus has come to set you free (John 8:36). It is possible to overcome!

THE PATH: WORKBOOK ACTIVITIES

We welcome you to start planning your ideal life today. Please read the following information and then use the following pages to describe your vision or dream in whatever manner is most effective for you.

Turn to page 11, "Free Write Your Dream/Vision," and follow the instructions.

Turn to page 12, "Create a Dream/Vision Board," and spend some time creating and reflecting on your Dream/Vision Board.

Turn to page 13, "Putting It All Together," and continue working on your Dream/Vision, and explore Biblical passages that will ignite your imagination.

Turn to page 14, "Journal," and share things you have learned, and things you want to change or maintain.

Turn to page 15, "Explore God's Word," to deepen your walk with God

Free Write Your Dream/Vision

A dream/vision can be a personal picture in your imagination that inspires possibilities for the future. Imagination is powerful. It is your God-given ability to be creative and form images in your mind and senses. Let's use the gift of your divinely inspired imagination and ability to dream, to envision your best, most satisfying, most ideal (not necessarily perfect) life.

To begin, settle in, take a deep breath, and quiet your mind. Slowly and simply enter into your divinely inspired imagination. Suppose for a moment that tonight you go to sleep and dream. The next day when you awake, your life is as you dreamed and is the best, most satisfying and most ideal (not necessarily perfect) life you can imagine. Allow yourself permission to explore, get creative, and dream! Write everything in detail.

What are you doing and what would your environment look like?

What components of your dream life already exist?

What would your schedule look like?

What would you be thinking and feeling?

What people would be around you?

What are you doing for your community (friends, church, job, neighborhood, etc.)?

Where is your faith and God in your dream/vision?

Action Plan: Read the story of Noah from the Bible to explore how faith and vision changed his life *(Genesis 6-9)*. Look for other people in the Bible to discover how they dealt with and experienced faith and vision (For example: Abraham, the Disciples, or others).

Create A Dream/Vision Board

Using your answers on the previous page,
write a summary statement of your Dream/Vision.

Now draw, write, and/or create a Dream/Vision board.
You can use this space to create your Dream/Vision board or
you can use a larger piece of paper or create it digitally. Be creative.

Action Plan: Check everything on your Dream/Vision Board and align it with God's Word. If you are uncertain, seek out a pastor, priest or other Christian to help.

Putting It All Together

Using the dream/vision board, simplify what you have been doing into a word or phrase and a Bible verse.

Choose a word or phrase:
What word or phrase resonates with you right now?

Look in the Bible or do an Internet search to help you understand your word or phrase more fully and see where it appears in Scripture.

Pick a life verse from the Bible.
A life verse is a verse from the Bible that speaks directly to your heart.

God wants you to use your divinely inspired imagination.

The Bible is filled with stories, imagery, figurative language, and metaphors. Our imagination allows us to deepen our relationship with God and see His plans for us. For example, He shared with Abraham that his decedents would be as vast as the stars *(Genesis 26:4)*.

Deepen your Biblical imagination.
Read John 15:1-8 and use your imagination to see the story.
Write what you see and experience.

Action Plan: Consider sharing the activities in Dare to Dream with someone close to you. Choose one next logical step to move you toward your dream.

Journal

What did you learn about yourself?

What are some things you want to change or keep the same?

Explore God's Word

Take the time to read each of these verses about Dreams/Vision.
Let us end this section with a prayer for you.
(Scan QR code below for a prayer.)

"For I know the plans I have for you," says the Lord.
"They are plans for good and not for disaster,
to give you a future and a hope."
Jeremiah 29:11

"Then, after doing all those things,
I will pour out my Spirit upon all people.
Your sons and daughters will prophesy.
Your old men will dream dreams,
and your young men will see visions."
Joel 2:28

"Then the Lord said to me,
'Write my answer plainly on tablets,
so that a runner can carry the correct message to others.
This vision is for a future time.
It describes the end, and it will be fulfilled.
If it seems slow in coming, wait patiently,
for it will surely take place.
It will not be delayed.'"
Habakkuk 2:2-3

"You didn't choose me. I chose you.
I appointed you to go and produce lasting fruit,
so that the Father will give you whatever you ask for, using my name."
John 15:16

"Now all glory to God, who is able,
through his mighty power at work within us,
to accomplish infinitely more than we might ask or think."
Ephesians 3:20

- *Scan the code with your mobile device for a prayer.*

Core Truth 2:

CONNECT WITH GOD

"Trust in the Lord with all your heart and lean not on your own understanding; in all your ways submit to Him, and He will make your paths straight."

Proverbs 3:5-6 (NIV)

WELCOME
to
CONNECT WITH GOD

The purpose of Connect With God is to help you understand God's character, nature, and love for you, and how you can hear from and connect with Him.

Scan the code with your mobile device for a video introducing Connect With God.

THE MAP: GOD'S WORD

The Bible is God speaking directly to you. It was penned by people through divine inspiration of God and is useful for every aspect of your life. It corrects you, teaches you, prepares you, and equips you to do every good work *(2 Timothy 3-16, 2 Peter 1:20-21)*.

Jesus explained that He is the vine, and believers in Christ are the branches. Through Jesus you have been pruned and purified. When you remain in Him, you will bear much fruit *(John 15:1-8)*. God desires for you to connect with Him through His Son Jesus Christ; in doing so, He will be with you as you walk through life. God says in His Word that He is love and He loves you with a never-ending love *(1 Corinthians 13)*. He is perfect: ever present, all knowing, and all powerful *(Psalms 46:1, 139:4, and 147:4-5)*. God forgives *(1 John 1:9)* and saves *(John 3:16)*.You were made in God's image to have a close relationship with Him and others *(Genesis 1:27, Matthew 22:37-39, John 13:34)*.

PRACTICAL STEPS FOR YOUR JOURNEY

THOUGHTS FOR THE JOURNEY:

God wants a relationship with you, and He desires you to want a relationship with Him.

Your relationship with God is developed in the same way that your human relationships are formed. You spend time together, ask questions, listen, and talk. The more time you spend praying and reading the Bible, the more you will understand God and feel connected to Him.

To meditate is to simply focus on, ponder, think, mutter, or speak quietly again and again *(Joshua 1:8)*. Meditation is biblical and aids in the anchoring of oneself in God's Word.

God is perfect, consisting of three, distinct, yet equal persons: our Heavenly Father, the only begotten Son Jesus Christ, and the Holy Spirit. This is the triune (3-in-1) God who is kind, compassionate, and loves you.

ACTIONS FOR THE JOURNEY:

- Recognize that you and all humanity have been created for relationship with God (See page 20 Ask Jesus to be your Lord and Savior).
- Strive to live a life of surrender...one in which you give your life, thoughts, heart, words, and actions over to God, being fully confident in Him, and allowing Him to lead every step of the way.
- Surrender to your loving God is a choice. You have freedom of choice.

ROADBLOCKS COMMON IN THE JOURNEY:

False beliefs about God	Self-righteousness	Pride
False beliefs about the Bible	Self-centeredness	Unforgiveness
Fear of not being in control	Self-loathing	Shame
Selfishness	Self-protectiveness	False Guilt

When you identify a roadblock, call on God to help you overcome that roadblock and choose a new path. Know that Jesus has come to set you free (John 8:36). It is possible to overcome!

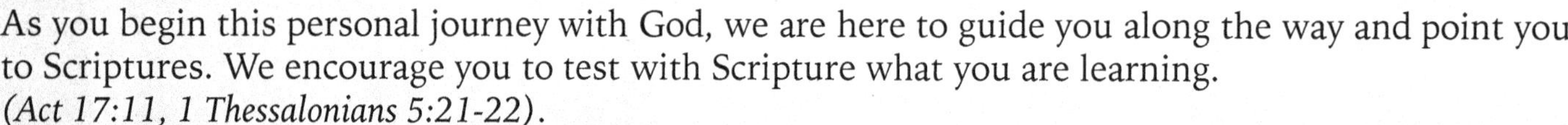

THE PATH: WORKBOOK ACTIVITIES

As you begin this personal journey with God, we are here to guide you along the way and point you to Scriptures. We encourage you to test with Scripture what you are learning. *(Act 17:11, 1 Thessalonians 5:21-22)*.

Turn to page 19, “People’s View of God,” to better understand who God is to you based on your experiences with God.

Turn to page 20, “Go to the Source,” to better understand that the Bible is Truth and God speaks to you personally. A better understanding of God will help you build a deeper relationship with Him.

Turn to page 21, “God is Triune (3-in1),” to better understand the nature, character, and attributes of God.

Turn to pages 22-23, “Ways to Hear from God,” and “Ways to Connect with God,” for Biblical understanding on hearing from and connecting with God.

Turn to pages 24-25, “The Power of STIL: Stillness,” and “The Power of STIL: Breath,” and follow the directions to complete the exercises.

Turn to page 26, “Journal,” and share things you have learned and things you would like to change or maintain.

Turn to page 27, “Explore God’s Word,” to deepen your walk with God.

People's View Of God

People view God in many ways. Below is a list of common opinions. Please look at the list and circle the ones you believe to be correct.

Loving/Generous

Approachable

Earthly Parents/Caregivers

Caring

Police Officer/Drill Sergeant

Genie who grants wishes

Punisher and Harsh Judge

Puppeteer - We are His puppets

Dangerous and Unjust

Hands-off/Uncaring

Reflect on who God is to you.
What narratives have you heard from others about God?

What experiences have you had personally that defined who God is to you?

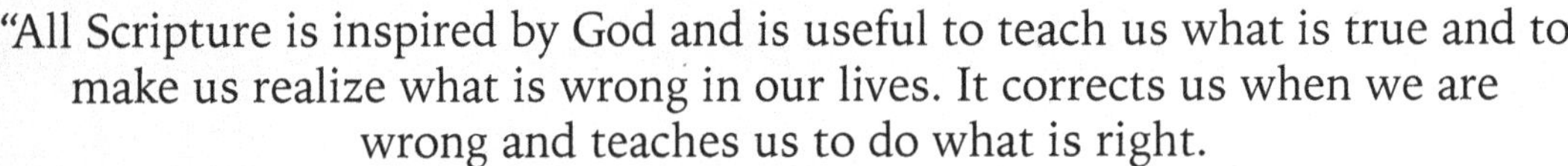

Go To The Source

You can trust that God is who He says He is.

"All Scripture is inspired by God and is useful to teach us what is true and to make us realize what is wrong in our lives. It corrects us when we are wrong and teaches us to do what is right.
God uses it to prepare and equip His people to do every good work."
2 Timothy 3:16-17

"Above all, you must realize that no prophecy in Scripture ever came from the prophet's own understanding, or from human initiative. No, those prophets were moved by the Holy Spirit, and they spoke from God."
2 Peter 1:20-21

God loves you and wants a relationship with you through His Son, the Lord Jesus Christ.
John 3:16, Romans 8:14-17, 1 John 3:1

He waits to be invited into your life.
John 1:12, Revelation 3:20

We encourage you to have a relationship with God beyond just knowing who He is. How do you build your relationship with God?

Ask Jesus to be your Lord and Savior.

If you are not certain you have a true relationship with Jesus Christ as your Lord and Savior, we invite you to join us in this video to pray a prayer of salvation.

God Is Triune (3-in-1)

You serve one God, who exists as three distinct and equal persons. The Trinity is God, your Heavenly Father; Jesus, the only begotten Son; and the Holy Spirit. Together they function as one divine being, sharing eternally and equally one nature, power, action, and will. This is the mystery of the Triune God.

God, the Heavenly Father
(Creator, Divine Ruler of All)
Ephesians 4:6

Jesus, the only begotten Son
(Perfect, Sinless, Savior)
John 3:16

Holy Spirit, guides into Truth
(Counselor, Comforter)
John14:16-17

God is your **CREATOR**: *Genesis 1:1*
God is **ONE**: *Deuteronomy 6:4*
God **PROTECTS**: *Psalm 5:11-12*
God is **EVER-PRESENT**: *Psalm 46:1*
God is **ETERNAL**: *Psalm 90:2*
God **RESCUES**: *Psalm 91:14-15*
God is **GOOD**: *Psalm 107:1*
God **GUIDES:** *Psalm 119:105*

God is **ALL-KNOWING**: *Psalm 139:4*
God is **ALL-POWERFUL**: *Psalm 147:4-5*
God is **UNCHANGEABLE**: *Malachi 3:6*
God **SAVES**: *John 3:16*
God is **LOVE**: *1Corinthians 13*
God **PROVIDES**: *Philippians 4:19*
God **CANNOT LIE**: *Titus 1:2*
God **FORGIVES**: *1 John 1:9*

Write any attributes of God, not listed, that are important to you.

Bottom line: God is **PERFECT** and beyond comprehension.

"'My thoughts are nothing like your thoughts,' says the LORD. 'And my ways are far beyond anything you could imagine. For just as the heavens are higher than the earth, so my ways are higher than your ways and my thoughts higher than your thoughts.'"
Isaiah 55:8-9

Ways To Hear From God

Take a look at the list of Ways to Hear From God and consider if any of them have ever spoken to you. As you begin to recall various ways in which God has spoken to you, please utilize the box below to record some of those ways. Expect God to teach, correct, clarify, reveal, and fill you with His grace, love, and forgiveness as you seek Him.

Still Small Voice

"And after the earthquake there was a fire, but the Lord was not in the fire.
And after the fire there was the sound of a gentle whisper."
1 Kings 19:12

Dreams/Vision

"Then, after doing all those things, I will pour out my Spirit upon all people.
Your sons and daughters will prophesy. Your old men will dream dreams,
and your young men will see visions."
Joel 2:28

Other People

"Plans go wrong for lack of advice; many advisers bring success."
Proverbs 15:22

Circumstances

"Now the Lord had arranged for a great fish to swallow Jonah. And Jonah was inside the fish for three days and three nights. Then Jonah prayed to the Lord his God from the fish's belly."
Jonah 1:17-2:1

Nature

"For ever since the world was created, people have seen the earth and sky. Through everything God made, they can clearly see his invisible qualities—His eternal power and divine nature. So they have no excuse for not knowing God."
Romans 1:20

Peace

"And let the peace that comes from Christ rule in your hearts. For as members of one body you are called to live in peace. And always be thankful."
Colossians 3:15

Prayer

"Always be joyful. Never stop praying. Be thankful in all circumstances,
for this is God's will for you who belong to Christ Jesus."
1 Thessalonians 5:16-18

Write out ways that God has spoken to you.

Ways To Connect With God

We encourage you to pause and reflect on whether you have truly connected with God in any of the methods listed below. Please use the box below to write down ways you have connected with God. Expect to find God and be transformed by Him as you seek Him.

Read The Bible Daily

"Study this Book of Instruction continually. Meditate on it day and night so you will be sure to obey everything written in it. Only then will you prosper and succeed in all you do."
Joshua 1:8

Speak The Word Over Your Life

"May the words of my mouth and the meditation of my heart be pleasing to you, O Lord, my rock and my redeemer."
Psalm 19:14

Praise And Worship

"Yet you are holy, enthroned on the praises of Israel."
Psalm 23:3

Join A Bible Study And Connect With Others

"He makes the whole body fit together perfectly. As each part does its own special work, it helps the other parts grow, so that the whole body is healthy and growing and full of love."
Ephesians 4:16

Join A Local Church

"And let us not neglect our meeting together, as some people do, but encourage one another, especially now that the day of His return is drawing near."
Hebrews 10:25

Act On The Word

"But don't just listen to God's word. You must do what it says. Otherwise, you are only fooling yourselves. "
James 1:22

Confess Regularly To Him And Pray

"But if we confess our sins to Him, He is faithful and just to forgive us our sins and to cleanse us from all wickedness."
1 John 1:9

Write out ways that you have connected with God.

The Power Of STIL: STILLNESS

"Let all that I am wait quietly before God, for my hope is in Him."
Psalm 62:5

1. Get comfortable and quiet, even if for a moment (*Psalm 46:10a*).
2. Stillness is the practice of quieting your mind from the cares of the day to focus only on God and His Word. Embrace the holy presence of the Lord (*Isaiah 6:1-4, Habakkuk 2:20*).
3. Imagine Him sitting with you. Invite God to talk to you. Let God gently speak to you (*1 Kings 19:12*).
4. Turn your eyes to Jesus Christ. See His finished work on the cross. Receive all the benefits, freedom, acceptance, grace and love of His finished work. Embrace all that He is, all that He has done, and all that He will continue to do for you. (*Psalm 103:2, Hebrew 12:2*).
5. When you are ready, continue on with your day, and do the next best thing that comes to mind that aligns with God's truth (*Philippians 1:6; 2:13*).

Feel free to sit in silence and think on the Lord. You can simply sit and enjoy the quiet, restful, presence of the Lord. You may also enjoy listening to quiet Christian music in the background. In these times of stillness, God often speaks. One common way is a spontaneous flow of thoughts. If you wish to capture any of those thoughts, have a pen and paper with you, write what you hear, and then check Scripture for accuracy or contact a trusted, mature Christian.

Now that you have practiced The Power of STIL: Stillness, describe your experience.

Look up and write down your favorite Bible verses on peace and stillness.

The Power Of STIL: BREATH

"Again he said, 'Peace be with you. As the Father has sent me, so I am sending you.'
Then he breathed on them and said, 'Receive the Holy Spirit'"
John 20:21-22

1. Get comfortable and quiet, even if for a moment (*Psalm 46:10a*).
2. Begin by breathing deeply through your nose (fill your belly as if it were a balloon), hold for just a moment, and then exhale deeply. Repeat as many times as needed.
3. When you inhale, see Jesus as your Breath of Life, breathing new life and what you need into you: His strength, His love, His peace, His wisdom, His healing, His forgiveness, His protection, His righteousness, His grace, His mercy (*Ephesians 3:14-20*).
4. When you exhale, breathe out your stress, troubles, and concerns; allow Jesus to take them (*1 Peter 5:7*).
5. Repeat until your thoughts, emotions, and body are at peace and you feel filled to the brim with the Breath of Jesus (*Ephesians 3:19*). Receive the comfort and counsel of the Holy Spirit.
6. As you close, let every breath you breathe be praise to the Lord (*Psalm 150:6*)
7. When you are ready, continue on with your day and do the next best thing that comes to mind that aligns with God's truth (*Philippians 1:6; 2:13*).

Now that you have practiced The Power of STIL: Breath, describe your experience.

Look up and write down your favorite Bible verses on rest and breath.

Action Plan: Allow the Lord's love to wash over you and receive a deeper understanding of Jesus Christ as your Lord and Savior (*John 3:16*).

Journal

What did you learn about who God is?

Now that you are more aware of who God is, has it changed how you view and experience Him? If so, explain below.

Write in detail all of the things that God has done for you.

What will you do to connect more deeply with God? (For example: read the Bible, pray, etc.)

Explore God's Word

Take the time to read each of these verses about Connect With God.

God is your **CREATOR**:
"In the beginning God created the heavens and the earth."
Genesis 1:1

God **PROTECTS**:
"But let all who take refuge in you rejoice; let them sing joyful praises forever.
Spread your protection over them, that all who love your name may be filled with joy.
For you bless the godly, O Lord; you surround them with your shield of love."
Psalm 5:11-12

God is **EVER-PRESENT**:
"Before the mountains were born, before you gave birth to the earth and the world,
from beginning to end, you are God."
Psalm 90:2

God is **ALL-POWERFUL**:
"He counts the stars and calls them all by name.
How great is our Lord! His power is absolute! His understanding is beyond comprehension!"
Psalm 147:4-5

God is **ALL-KNOWING**:
"You know what I am going to say even before I say it, Lord."
Psalm 139:4

God is your **PROVIDER**:
"Look at the birds. They don't plant or harvest or store food in barns, for your heavenly Father feeds them. And aren't you far more valuable to Him than they are?"
Matthew 6:26

God is **TRIUNE**:
"May the grace of the Lord Jesus Christ, the love of God,
and the fellowship of the Holy Spirit be with you all."
2 Corinthians 13:14

Scan the code with your mobile device for a prayer.

Core Truth 3:

KNOW WHO YOU ARE

"For it was You who created my inward parts;
You knit me together in my mother's womb.
I will praise You because I have been fearfully and wonderfully made."
Psalm 139:13-14

WELCOME
to
KNOW WHO YOU ARE

The purpose of Know Who You Are is to help you recognize and honor your unique skills, talents, and abilities that are God-given and to know who you are in Christ through His gift of salvation.

Scan the code with your mobile device for a video introducing Know Who You Are

THE MAP: GOD'S WORD

God made you with a variety of skills and abilities, which He wants you to discover and appreciate *(Psalm 139:13-14, Romans 12)*. As a result of God's work, He invites you to find rest in Him *(Matthew 11:28-30)*. Jesus Christ, the author and perfecter of your faith, wants you to look to Him constantly *(Hebrews 12:2)*, and meditate (focus, ponder) on His Word *(Psalm 1:2-3)*.

God desires you to acknowledge that His Son, Jesus Christ, died so that you might experience forgiveness of sin, eternal life, and all the benefits that come with being a Christian *(Psalm 103:2)*. Benefits include assurance that He will supply all your needs *(Philippians 4:19)*, acceptance, and a promise that He will not abandon, betray, or forsake you *(Hebrews 13:5b)*. You have your identity in Christ. You're His masterpiece, the apple of His eye, a Citizen of Heaven, and a child of God *(John 1:12)*, and you've been designed with a purpose, a hope, and a future *(Jeremiah 29:11)*.

PRACTICAL STEPS FOR YOUR JOURNEY

THOUGHTS FOR THE JOURNEY:

You are loved, unique, and belong to God *(Romans 1:6)*.

God loves you with an everlasting love *(Jeremiah 31:3)*. If you have accepted Jesus Christ as your Lord and Savior, you are now filled with His resurrection power, and are a new creature *(1 Peter 1:3, Romans 6:4)*, and you can do all things through Christ who strengthens you *(Philippians 4:13)*.

Know God created you to be uniquely you. He is the source of your gifts, skills, talents, and abilities. He is the potter, and you are the clay *(Isaiah 64:8)*.

The more you know who you are in Christ, the easier it is for Him to transform and fill you with His love, His knowledge, and His all-encompassing peace *(Romans 12:1-2)*.

ACTIONS FOR THE JOURNEY:

- Name and live out your strengths, passions, skills, and talents, and utilize them more.
- Name and respect your value system (values are dearly held principles that help guide the way you live your life).
- Recognize, learn, and practice practical ways God has given you to take care of your spirit, soul, and body.
- Take hold of the truth that Jesus Christ lives in you because of the gift of salvation and embrace that you have His peace *(Romans 5:1, Colossians 1:27)*.

ROADBLOCKS COMMON IN THE JOURNEY:

Believing that you are a failure
Worthless
Not good enough or unlovable
Insecurity
Inferiority
Fear
Shame
False Guilt
Living contrary to your values
Exhaustion/Fatigue
Being overwhelmed
Distractions
Focusing on the negative
Not recognizing your strengths
Not taking care of yourself
Don't know who you are in Christ

When you identify a roadblock, call on God to help you overcome that roadblock and choose a new path. Know that Jesus has come to set you free (John 8:36). It is possible to overcome!

THE PATH: WORKBOOK ACTIVITIES

We welcome you to start knowing who you are today.

Turn to page 31, "What Defines You?," and "Who Are YOU?," follow the instructions and fill out as much as you can right now.

Turn to pages 32-34, "Core Values," "Strengths," and "Take Care of Yourself," read over the sheets and follow the instructions.

Turn to page 35, "The Power of STIL: Meditation," and follow the instructions to learn how to Biblically meditate.

Turn to page 36, "Who I am In Christ," read through the list, believe and breathe in the truth of His love and who He says you are.

Turn to page 37, "The Joy of Being in Christ," "Ask Me Who I Am," and "Distractions," to deepen who you are in Christ and remove distractions that keep you from thriving.

Turn to page 38, "Journal," and share things you have learned and things you want to change or maintain.

Turn to page 39, "Explore God's Word," to deepen your walk with God.

What Defines You?

List all of your identifications, roles (such as parent, student, teacher), degrees, diagnoses, or labels you have been given.

Your labels and roles may have meaning, but they don't need to define you. Your true worth and value is defined by God through Jesus Christ. You are righteous, holy, blessed, redeemed, dearly loved, and so much more. Celebrate and anchor yourself in how God fearfully and wonderfully made you.

Who Are YOU?

What are your hobbies and interests?

What brings you joy?

What are you proud of that you have accomplished?

What are your desires and passions?

What has shaped you? (For example: people, places, things, ideas)

How do you overcome obstacles and challenges?

List all the people, places, and things for which you are grateful.

Core Values

Core Values are your deeply-held principles, standards, and personal judgments as to what you hold important in life.

What are your core values?
Read through the list of values; then circle five that reflect your highest values.

Adventure
Advancement
Affection
Appreciation
Authenticity
Balance
Beauty
Career
Caring
Change
Charisma
Clarity
Commonality
Communication
Compassion
Connection
Contentment
Contributing
Cooperation
Courage
Creativity
Discipline
Diversity
Effectiveness
Encouragement
Enjoyment
Entertaining
Entrepreneurial
Equity
Excellence
Excitement

Facilitation
Faith
Family
Finances
Finesse
Fitness
Forgiveness
Freedom
Fun-loving
Friendship
Generosity
Giving people a chance
Goodness
Grace
Gratitude
Growth
Happiness
Harmony
Home
Honesty
Hope
Humor
Independence
Innovation
Integrity
Intelligence
Invention
Involvement
Kindness
Knowledge
Leadership

Learning
Love
Loyalty
Openness
Optimism
Order
Patience
Peace
People
Personal development
Power
Preparedness
Pride in your work
Professionalism
Prosperity
Quality
Reciprocity
Relationship
Respect
Security
Self-respect
Stewardship
Strength
Success
Teamwork
Trusting your gut
Wealth
Wellness
Willingness
Wisdom
Work/Life balance

Add any of your Core Values not listed here ______________________________

Action Plan: Explore your core values and journal when you see yourself making decisions based on these values. When you live in harmony with your Core Values, you are at your most secure.

Strengths

What are your strengths?
Read through the list of strengths; then circle at least seven that describe you.

Accurate
Action-oriented
Adventurous
Ambitious
Analytical
Appreciative
Artistic
Assertive
Athletic
Authentic
Boldness
Bravery
Caring
Clever
Compassionate
Communicative
Confident
Considerate
Courageous
Creative
Curious
Decisive
Dedicated
Deliberate
Detail-oriented
Determined
Disciplined
Educated
Empathetic
Energetic
Entertaining
Enthusiastic
Fair
Flexible
Focused
Friendly
Generous
Grateful
Helpful
Honest
Hopeful
Humble
Humorous
Idealistic
Independent
Ingenious
Industrious
Inquisitive
Inspirational
Intelligent
Kind
Knowledgeable
Leading
Lively
Logical
Lovely
Merciful
Modest
Moral
Motivated
Observant
Optimistic
Open-minded
Orderly
Original
Organized
Outgoing
Patient
Peaceful
Perseverance
Persuasive
Persistent
Practical
Precise
Problem-solving
Prudent
Quick-witted
Resourceful
Respectful
Responsible
Self-assured
Self-controlled
Serious
Spiritual
Spontaneous
Social
Straightforward
Strategic
Tactful
Team-oriented
Thoughtful
Thrifty
Tolerant
Trustworthy
Versatile
Visionary
Warm
Welcoming
Wise

Add any of your strengths not listed here ______________________________

Action Plan: Explore each of your strengths. Take each one and journal specific details and times that you are demonstrating these qualities.

Take Care Of Yourself

How do you take care of yourself? Read the lists below and circle the things that you do.

ADVENTURE
- explore a new hobby
- book a weekend getaway
- find something free to do in your area
- go on a picnic
- learn a new language

BOUNDARIES
- say "no" to something (or someone)
- consider who you follow in social media
- go to bed 30 minutes early
- sleep in
- take a whole day to do nothing

CONNECT
- give someone a hug
- call someone you care about
- meet a friend for coffee/tea
- smile at a stranger on the street
- volunteer for a cause you care about

ELECTRONICS/SOCIAL MEDIA
- follow inspirational people online
- curl up with a blanket and stream a movie
- make a board with inspiring quotes
- make a playlist of songs that uplift you
- create a playlist of worship music

EXERCISE/MOVEMENT
- go to your favorite workout class
- take a walk or hike
- dance in your living room
- play frisbee golf with a friend
- play an outside sport

SPA/RELAX
- take a bath
- give yourself a manicure/pedicure
- do 5 minutes of deep breathing
- turn your phone off
- snuggle your dog/cat

MEALS/FOOD
- drink more water
- eat something yummy
- eat your lunch/dinner away from screens
- get your favorite coffee/latte/mocha
- try a new restaurant

WRITING/CREATING
- journal
- make a gratitude list
- write a letter or send an email
- paint a picture or create art
- write a poem or create a song

SPIRITUAL
- pray
- meditate on God's Word and who He is
- join a Bible study
- attend a church service
- listen to worship music

WHAT DO YOU DO TO TAKE CARE OF YOURSELF?

God Care: Allow God's Word to fill you with love, value, strength, and care.

Action Plan: Star two ways you take care of yourself and are willing to do this week.
Ask someone you trust what they do to take care of themselves.

The Power Of STIL: MEDITATION

"But they delight in the law of the LORD, meditating on it day and night.
They are like trees planted along the riverbank, bearing fruit each season.
Their leaves never wither, and they prosper in all they do."
Psalm 1:2-3

1. Get comfortable and quiet, even if for a moment *(Psalm 46:10a)*.
2. Look up a Scripture that speaks to you at this time *(2 Timothy 3:16)*.
3. Slowly, carefully, and thoroughly read, think, and reflect on each word.
4. Repeat the Scripture over and over. To meditate is to simply focus on, ponder, think, mutter, or speak quietly again and again *(Joshua 1:8)*.
5. Use your divinely inspired imagination to visualize and picture yourself-spirit-soul-body in the actual Scripture, in the presence of God, or somewhere special where you and God meet *(Psalm 145:5; 1 Thessalonians 5:23)*.
6. Pause and reflect on what God is speaking and showing you *(Psalm 34:8)*.
7. When you are ready, continue on with your day and do the next best thing that comes to mind that aligns with God's truth *(Philippians 1:6; 2:13)*.

Now that you have practiced the Power of STIL: Meditation, describe your experience.

Who I Am In Christ

If you have accepted Jesus Christ as your Lord and Savior you have been crucified with Christ. You belong and are permanently adopted into His family. (Galatians 2:20-21, 3:27). Therefore, you now have His resurrection power and all the benefits of being in Christ as your very own (Romans 6:4). Read through and breathe in God's truth about who you really are in Christ.

I am tenderly loved by God *(Jeremiah 31:3).*
I am the light of the world *(Matthew 5:14).*
I am a child of God *(John 1:12).*
I am loved by God and He gave His only begotten Son for me *(John 3:16).*
I am protected *(John 10:28).*
I am at peace with God *(John 14:27).*
I am Christ's friend *(John 15:15).*
I am chosen by Christ to bear fruit *(John 15:16).*
I am a personal witness of Christ *(Acts 1:8).*
I am dead to sin *(Romans 1:12).*
I am reconciled to God *(Romans 5:11).*
I am not condemned by God *(Romans 8:1).*
I am set free *(Romans 8:2).*
I am a joint-heir with Christ, sharing His inheritance with Him *(Romans 8:17).*
I know all things are working together for my good because I love God *(Romans 8:28).*
I am more than a conqueror *(Romans 8:37).*
I am victorious *(1 Corinthians 15:57).*
I am Christ's ambassador *(2 Corinthians 5:20).*
I am a child of God and at one with others in His family *(Galatians 3:26, 28).*
I am saved by grace through faith *(Ephesians 2:8-9).*
I am secure *(Ephesians 2:20).*
I am a holy temple and dwelling place for the Holy Spirit *(Ephesians 2:22).*
I am completed by God *(Ephesians 3:19).*
I am righteous and holy *(Ephesians 4:24).*
I am confident that the good work God has begun in me will be perfected *(Philippians 1:6).*
I am a citizen of heaven *(Philippians 3:20).*
I am completely forgiven *(Colossians 1:14).*
I am chosen by God, holy, and dearly loved *(Colossians 3:12).*
I am a child of the light *(1 Thessalonians 5:5).*
I am holy, and I share in God's heavenly calling *(Hebrews 3:1).*
I am not alone *(Hebrews 13:5).*
I am born again through the living and enduring Word of God *(1 Peter 1:23).*
I am healed from sin and its effects *(1 Peter 2:24).*
I am an overcomer *(1 John 5:4).*
I am born of God, and the devil cannot touch me *(1 John 5:18).*

Action Plan: Meditate, using all your five senses and imagination; see and embrace who you are in Christ (*Psalm 1:2*).

The Joy Of Being In Christ

Being in Christ you have all of the following:

Forgiveness
(He has given you complete and total forgiveness of your sins)
John 3:16

Acceptance
(He will never abandon, betray or reject you)
Romans 5:17

Identity
(You are His masterpiece, A Citizen of Heaven, Child of God)
John 1:12

Security
(He supplies all of your needs)
Philippians 4:19

Purpose
(He built you with certain gifts to give you a future and a hope)
Jeremiah 29:11

Ask Me Who I Am

Go back to Who I Am In Christ to complete this sentence.

"I am ______________________________ because

God says I am ______________________________."

Distractions

Now that you know more about God and who you are, what distractions may be keeping you from thriving? (For example: video games, volunteering excessively, social media, etc.)

Action Plan: Hand each of your distractions to God.
Ask Him to give you solutions to live in better balance.

Journal

Take a moment to reflect on what you have learned about yourself and who you are in Christ. Summarize your values and strengths.

Explore God's Word

Below are some Scriptures on who you are in Christ. Meditate on these Scriptures. In addition, look up, write down, and meditate on all the Scriptures where you find the words "In Christ" and Jesus saying "I am." Find the ones that bring you closer to God and to knowing who you are in Him.

I am the light of the world.
"You are the light of the world—like a city on a hilltop that cannot be hidden."
Matthew 5:14

I am loved by God and He gave His only begotten Son for me.
"For this is how God loved the world: He gave His only begotten Son, so that everyone who believes in Him will not perish but have eternal life."
John 3:16

I am securely His.
"I give them eternal life, and they will never perish. No one can snatch them away from me, for my Father has given them to me, and He is more powerful than anyone else. No one can snatch them from the Father's hand."
John 10:28-29

I am not condemned by God.
"So now there is no condemnation for those who belong to Christ Jesus."
Romans 8:1

I am more than a conqueror.
"Now, despite all these things, overwhelming victory is ours through Christ, who loved us."
Romans 8:37

I am saved by grace through faith.
"God saved you by His grace when you believed. And you can't take credit for this; it is a gift from God. Salvation is not a reward for the good things we have done, so none of us can boast about it."
Ephesians 2:8-9

I am born of God, and the devil can not touch me.
"We know that God's children do not make a practice of sinning, for God's Son holds them securely, and the evil one cannot touch them."
1 John 5:18

- *Scan the code with your mobile device for a prayer.*

Core Truth 4:

THRIVE INSIDE AND OUT

"Do not be anxious about anything, but in every situation, by prayer and petition, with thanksgiving, present your requests to God. And the peace of God, which transcends all understanding, will guard your hearts and your minds in Christ Jesus."

Philippians 4:6-7

WELCOME
to
THRIVE INSIDE AND OUT

The purpose of Thrive Inside and Out is to help you live a Spirit-led life by allowing God into deeper levels of your thoughts, actions, feelings, words, behavior, and choices.

Scan the code with your mobile device for a video introducing Thrive Inside And Out

THE MAP: GOD'S WORD

God says in His Word that you are made up of three parts: spirit, soul, and body *(1 Thessalonians 5:23)*. Your spirit (the part that connects and communicates with God) and your soul (mind, will, emotions, and imagination) are contained in your physical body *(2 Corinthians 4:16, 3 John 1:2)*. God is Spirit, and He wants you to connect with Him through your spirit *(John 4:24)*. When you accept Jesus as your Lord and Savior, He joins with your spirit, makes you a new creation perfected in Christ, and seals you for all eternity with the Holy Spirit *(John 1:12, 2 Corinthians 1:21-22, 2 Corinthians 5:17, Ephesians 4:30)*.

The purpose of the Christian life is to walk with God and become more like Christ. One part of living a Christ-centered life is choosing to link and move in alignment in these three areas of spirit, soul, and body, with your spirit taking the lead. This is living a Spirit-led life *(Galatians 5:18, 25)*. You are not alone on this journey. When you call Jesus your Lord and Savior, your body becomes the dwelling place of the Holy Spirit with Christ living in you *(Galatians 2:20)*. You can now connect directly to God. Through Christ you can boldly come before His throne to receive mercy, find grace, and have help in all areas of your life *(Hebrews 4:16)*. He wants you to put all your worries on Him, because He cares for you *(1 Peter 5:7)*, and to experience His unshakable peace *(John 14:27)* and forgiveness *(1 John 1:9)*.

PRACTICAL STEPS FOR YOUR JOURNEY

THOUGHTS FOR THE JOURNEY:

You were created in the image of God *(Genesis 1:27)*. He has thoughts, emotions, actions and words. Therefore, you have them as well.

God says your body is His temple. He desires you to care for it *(1 Corinthians 6:19-20)*.

Thoughts aligned with God's will are true and lovely *(Philippians 4:8-9)*.

Emotions aligned with God's will are peaceful and contented *(John 14:27)*.

Behaviors aligned with God's will are kind, gentle, and self-controlled *(Galatians 5:22-23)*.

Words aligned with God's will encourage, instruct, and build up *(Ephesians 4:29)*.

ACTIONS FOR THE JOURNEY:

- Recognize when your soul and body are out of alignment with your spirit.
- Allow the fruit of the Spirit (love, joy, peace, patience, kindness, goodness, faithfulness, gentleness and self-control) and Scripture to dwell in your soul *(Galatians 5:22)*.
- Create a habit of being in the present moment and check how your body, thoughts, emotions, words, and behaviors are doing.
- He understands that you may get exhausted and overwhelmed at times. As a result, notice when your body and soul are stressed. Take time for self-care and rest *(1 Corinthians 6:19-20)*.
- Know that while on this earth, Jesus experienced everything you experience and did not sin. He has great compassion for you and your story *(Hebrews 4:15-16)*.
- When you make a misstep, which you will, seek and receive His forgiveness and start anew *(Hebrews 8:12)*. Consistently choose to forgive yourself and others as Christ forgave you *(Ephesians 4:32)*. Because of the finished work of Christ and your relationship with him, you are forgiven, accepted, loved, and made new *(John 3:3-6, Romans 5:1, Colossians 1:21-22, 1 John 4:9-11)*.

ROADBLOCKS COMMON IN THE JOURNEY:

Unforgiveness	Fear	Feeling inadequate
Bitterness	Resentment	Pride
Insecurity	Feeling unworthy	Being Passive
Inferiority	Feeling unlovable	Being Impulsive

When you identify a roadblock, call on God to help you overcome that roadblock and choose a new path. Know that Jesus has come to set you free (John 8:36). It is possible to overcome!

THE PATH: WORKBOOK ACTIVITIES

Turn to page 43, "Thrive Inside and Out: Three Part Being," read and answer the question.

Turn to pages 44-45, "The Power of STIL: Cast Your Cares," and "Cast Your Care Worksheet," follow the instructions for the meditation then reflect and answer the questions about your meditation.

Turn to pages 46-47, "Thriving Body,"and "The Power of STIL: Body," read and answer the questions about how your body responds to stress and how to use meditation for your body.

Turn to pages 48-49, "Thriving Body/The Limbic System," read and answer the questions.

Turn to pages 50-59, Thriving Thoughts, Emotions, Words, Behaviors. Follow the instructions to learn and practice thriving in all these areas.

Turn to pages 60-61, "The Power of STIL: Search," and "The Power of STIL: Confession and Forgiveness," follow the instructions for the meditation.

Turn to pages 62-63, "Effortlessly Change Your Situation," complete and reflect on how God can change your situation.

Turn to pages 64-65, "Journal," and "Explore God's Word," share things you have learned, things you want to change or maintain, and read Scriptures to deepen your walk with God.

Thrive Inside And Out: THREE-PART BEING

"Now may the God of peace make you holy in every way, and may your whole spirit and soul and body be kept blameless until our Lord Jesus Christ comes again."
1 Thessalonians 5:23

God says in His Word that you are made up of three parts: spirit, soul, and body *(1 Thessalonians 5:23)*. Your spirit (the part that connects and communicates with God) and your soul (mind, will, emotions, and imagination) are contained in your physical body *(2 Corinthians 4:16, 3 John 1:2)*. God is Spirit, and He wants you to connect with Him through your spirit *(John 4:24)*. When you accept Jesus as your Lord and Savior, He joins with your spirit, makes you a new creation perfected in Christ, and seals you for all eternity with the Holy Spirit *(John 1:12, 2 Corinthians 1:21-22, 2 Corinthians 5:17, Ephesians 4:30)*.

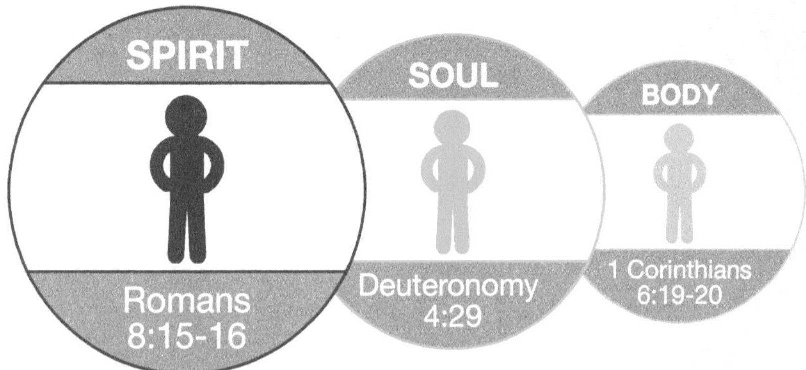

Spirit	Soul	Body
part of the inward person that connects and communicates with God *1 Corinthians 2:11-12*	part of the inward person that includes your mind, will, emotions, and imagination *Hebrews 4:12*	outward physical being that is mortal *2 Corinthians 4:16*

All Three Parts Matter:

Ask yourself what part of you is leading: your spirit, soul or body? The aim is to lead a life led by the Spirit *(Galatians 5:18, 25)*. This means choosing what God wants for you and your life, rather than what your soul and body want. To live an authentic, unified life is to live a life in which your spirit, soul, and body are in harmony. Becoming more Christ-like and Spirit-led is a life-long process and daily choice. God understands this struggle and tells you not to fear or worry *(Isaiah 35:4)*. His grace is sufficient; His mercies are new every morning *(Lamentations 3:22-23, 2 Corinthians 12:9)*. When you make a misstep,(which you will), ask, seek, and receive His love and forgiveness, and start anew *(Matthew 7:7-12, Hebrews 8:12)*. Keep your hope in the Lord *(Isaiah 40:29-31, Roman 15:13, Galatians 6:9, James 1:12)*.

What part (spirit, soul, and body) of you tends to lead your life most often? What steps can you take to align your spirit, soul, and body?

The Power Of STIL: CAST YOUR CARES

"Give all your worries and cares to God, for He cares about you."
1 Peter 5:7

1. Get comfortable and quiet, even if for a moment (*Psalm 46:10a*).
2. Use your imagination to see yourself standing in front of Jesus with his hands open to you.
3. Ask Jesus to help you search and become aware of your soul (mind, emotions, will, and imagination); look for any area of hurt, stress, or anxious thoughts (*Psalm 139:23, Matthew 11:28-30, John 14:1*).
4. For each thing that comes to mind that is causing you hurt, stress, or anxious thoughts visualize yourself giving it to Jesus once and for all (*1 Peter 5:7*).
5. For each care you hand to Jesus, see Him handing you back what you need: His love, grace, healing, strength, peace, wisdom, mercy, etc.(*Isaiah 41:10, Colossians 3:15, Philippians 2:5, James 1:5*). Believe and receive what Jesus hands back to you (*Matthew 21:22*).
6. When you are ready, continue on with your day and do the next best thing that comes to mind that aligns with God's truth (*Philippians 1:6; 2:13*).

Now that you have practiced the Power of STIL: Cast Your Cares, describe your experience.

Cast Your Cares Worksheet

"Give all your worries and cares to God, for He cares about you."
1 Peter 5:7

List all of your cares and see them being handed to Jesus.

What did you receive back from Him and His Word regarding each care?

Thriving Body

"Don't you realize that your body is the temple of the Holy Spirit, who lives in you and was given to you by God? You do not belong to yourself, for God bought you with a high price. So you must honor God with your body."
1 Corinthians 6:19-20

What does God say about your body?

In the New Testament, your body is referred to as a temple. In the Old Testament, the temple was a physical, sacred meeting place where the Israelites would meet with God. When you call Jesus your Lord and Savior, your body becomes the dwelling place of the Holy Spirit with Christ living in you *(Galatians 2:20)*. You can now connect directly to God. God cares about your body and wants you to care for it as well *(Romans 6:13, Romans 12:1)*. This is why He gave the Biblical command to Sabbath, or in Hebrew meaning to stop, for a day each week and as you need *(Exodus 20:8-11, Hebrews 4:9-10)*. Jesus took care of his spirit, soul, and body. He honored the Sabbath *(Mark 1:35)*. Your body tells you many things about what you need, including relief from stress. Stress in this life is inevitable *(James 1:2-4)*. He knows you need Him and the Sabbath. Understand and pay attention to your body, to know how this world and your thoughts are impacting your physical body.

Common Ways Your Body Responds to Stress

Butterflies	Restless/jittery	Heart racing	Sluggish
Stomachache	Adrenaline overload	Rapid breathing	Frozen
Nauseous	Out of control	Can't think	Disconnected
Heavy	Easily startled	Headache	Insomnia
Warm	Tense muscles	Overeating/undereating	Sleeping too much/too little
Clammy	Clumsy	Exhaustion	Nightmares

How does your body respond to stress?

How does your body feel when it is calm?

How can you Sabbath (stop) and keep your body physically healthy?

Action Plan: Look in the Bible for verses that talk about your body. Recognize when your body has a need. Pause, use the Power of STIL, and do the next best thing that aligns with God's truth.

The Power Of STIL: BODY

"You made all the delicate, inner parts of my body and
knit me together in my mother's womb."
Psalm 139:13

1. Get comfortable and quiet, even if for a moment (*Psalm 46:10a*).
2. Begin by slowly becoming aware and scanning each part of your body. Start at the top of your head and go the bottom of your feet.
3. Become aware of stress, tension, and what your body is telling you.
4. Anywhere you feel stress, tension, or pain, shake or move to let it all out; see yourself giving all your body's stress, tension, or pain to Jesus (*1 Peter 5:7*).
5. Receive from Jesus His peace (*John 14:27*) and His comfort (*2 Corinthians 1:3*)
6. Experience Him pouring His healing balm (anointing oil) over you from the top of your head to the bottom of your feet (*Psalm 23:5b, 1 Peter 2:24*).
7. Rest and breathe in the calm, peace, and love of Jesus until your body feels refreshed (*Job 33:4, Joel 2:25-26*).
8. When you are ready, continue on with your day and do the next best thing that comes to mind that aligns with God's truth (*Philippians 1:6; 2:13*).

Now that you have practiced the Power of STIL: Body, describe your experience.

Thriving Body/Limbic System

"I am leaving you with a gift—peace of mind and heart. And the peace I give is a gift the world cannot give. So don't be troubled or afraid."
John 14:27

God created your body and brain to work together for your protection and for your good. Simply, you have a thinking, choice-making, and an emotional brain that are part of your body.

What is the Limbic System?

When you perceive danger, real or imagined, your emotional brain, limbic system, is designed to help your body physically respond to keep you safe. That danger, real or imagined, is called a trigger. The system of response to danger is called flight, fight, or freeze. When its activated your body responds automatically without you thinking. For example, your heartbeat increases, hormones are released, and your pupils dilate. If you unexpectedly see a bear or a snake you may be ready to run, attack or become paralyzed. You are focused on safety and surviving. Unless safety is in question, be careful making decisions in this state. When you are triggered, even if there is no real danger, this automatic system will activate and impair your ability to access your soul and spirit.

How do I manage my thinking, choice-making, and emotional brain?

Calming down this activated system is important, especially if there is no real immediate danger. When you pause, breathe, and care for yourself, your thinking brain can re-engage. When you are calmer, you can then access both your soul and spirit. This gives you the ability to realistically evaluate the situation and choose how you want to move forward.

Limbic System

Prefrontal Cortex
Thinking Brain

Amygdala
Emotional Brain

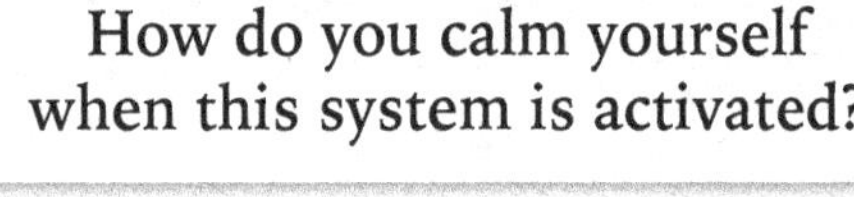

How do you calm yourself when this system is activated?

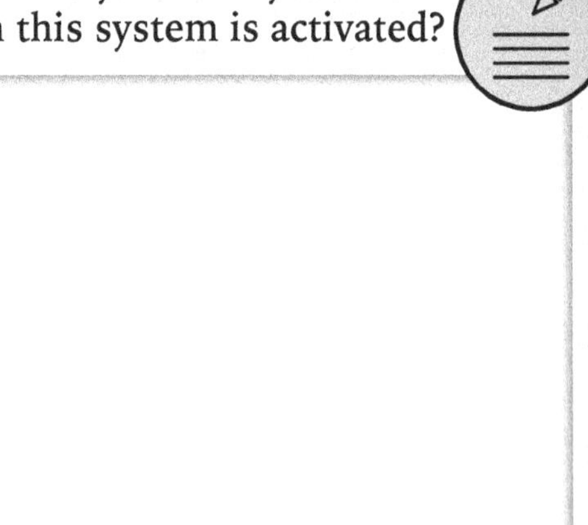

Some practical ways to help when you are afraid or overwhelmed: Sing a song, pray, take a break, move your body, smell something pleasing, listen to music, cuddle up in a fuzzy blanket, or fidget with something.

Action Plan: Make a list of the things that can practically help you with your triggers and fears.

Thriving Body/Limbic System

What does God Say about fear?

God created the Limbic System to help you recognize and respond to danger. The emotion tied with this system is often fear because it causes you to pay attention and act. Fear is necessary and good because it keeps you safe. You can walk in faith and experience fear. However, you don't want fear to control you. When you experience fear, God is your solution. God says in His Word He is with you when you are afraid (*Deuteronomy 31:6, Isaiah 41:10, Psalms 27:1, 46:1-3, 56:3-4, 91 Luke 14:27, Philippians 4:6-7, 2 Timothy 1:7*). When you experience fear, breathe, connect to God to calm your nervous system, and seek His wisdom (*Job 33:4, James 1:5*). God's perfect love casts out all fear (*1 John 4:18*).

What are your triggers?

What are your current fears?

How do you typically respond to fear or stress?

How can God be the solution to your triggers and fears?

"Don't be afraid, for I am with you. Don't be discouraged, for I am your God.
I will strengthen you and help you. I will hold you up with my victorious right hand."
Isaiah 41:10

Action Plan: Look up, write down, and meditate on Scriptures that can help you when you are overwhelmed and fearful.

Thriving Thoughts

"And now, dear brothers and sisters, one final thing. Fix your thoughts on what is true, and honorable, and right, and pure, and lovely, and admirable. Think about things that are excellent and worthy of praise. Keep putting into practice all you learned and received from me—everything you heard from me and saw me doing. Then the God of peace will be with you."

Philippians 4:8-9

What does God say about your thoughts?

God cares about your thought life. He wants you to be aware of and take care of your mind *(Proverbs 4:23)*. Your thoughts create emotions, and emotions create action. God says to take captive every thought *(2 Corinthians 10:3-6)*. You can choose your thoughts *(Deuteronomy 30:19)*, and you have the ability to renew your mind *(Romans 12:2)*. Your thoughts influence every aspect of your life. Thoughts build on themselves. The more you think negatively, the more negative thoughts. The more you think positively, the more positive thoughts *(Philippians 4:8)*.

You can choose your thoughts

Unhelpful Thoughts	Helpful Thoughts
Predicting the future negatively	Grounded in God's Word
Thinking the worst outcome	Truthful, hopeful, thankful and prayerful
Mind-reading	Open to many ideas and perspectives
Assuming	See solutions, not just the problem
All or nothing thinking	Believe the best in self and others
Jumping to conclusions	Allow for growth in opportunities
Perfectionism	Based on fact and common sense
Unforgiveness	Filled with knowledge/discernment
Failure/unlovable	Filled with understanding
Judgmental	Filled with wisdom

What thoughts do you struggle with that are unhelpful?

What other thoughts can you add that are helpful?

Action Plan: Look in the Bible for verses that address your thoughts.
Recognize when you are thinking in an unhelpful way, pause, use the Power of STIL, and do the new way.

Effortlessly Change Your Thinking

When you are experiencing thoughts that are unhelpful, invite God into your area of need. Walk through the steps in the worksheet below to help restore your thinking. Embrace God's Word as Him speaking to you. Accept the love God has for you. Trust in the grace, forgiveness, and mercy of Jesus Christ. Seek the counsel and comfort of the Holy Spirit. When you fully surrender to God, He will transform you from the inside out. This is effortless change.

REST *(Matthew 11:28-30)*
Pause and be still. Breathe. Invite God into the situation.
Stay here until you can respond and not react.

What is the situation?

RECOGNIZE *(Psalm 139:23-24)*
Become aware of your thoughts. Be kind to yourself in this reflection. Approach yourself and the situation with honesty, compassion, curiosity, courage, grace, and forgiveness.

What thoughts are you experiencing?

RENEW *(Romans 12:2)*
Ask God what you need right now to heal, renew, and transform your thoughts.
Use the Bible, Prayer, and (if helpful) the Power of STIL.

What Biblical and practical wisdom is God revealing to you?
What are your choices?

RESTORE *(Isaiah 40:31)*
Believe, receive, and act on what you have learned from God and His Word.
Honor God while you respect and love yourself and others.

Now that you have rested, recognized, and renewed, how do you want to Biblically and practically move forward to live a more Spirit-led life?

"Each time he said, 'My grace is all you need. My power works best in weakness.' So now I am glad to boast about my weaknesses, so that the power of Christ can work through me."
2 Corinthians 12:9

Thriving Emotions

"We know how much God loves us, and we have put our trust in his love. God is love, and all who live in love live in God, and God lives in them."
1 John 4:16

What does God say about emotions?

God is the creator of all and called His creation good (*Genesis 1:31*). He created and experiences emotions such as: Grief (*Genesis 6:6*); Jealousy (*Exodus 20:5*); Anger *(Psalm 7:11)*; Laughter (*Psalm 37:13*); Compassion (*Psalm 135:14*); Hate (*Proverbs 6:16*); and Joy (*Zephaniah 3:17*). God's emotions are consistent with who He is: loving, sinless, reliable, predictable, stable, and they flow from His perfection. Jesus recognized and joined with people's emotions and experiences (*John 4:4-26, 20:24-29*). Together, Jesus and you, can make a way for you to cope, care for your emotions, and make wise decisions. As Jesus is, so are you in the world (*1 John 4:17*).

Jesus showed emotions:

Jesus had compassion. *Matthew 14:14*
Jesus expressed anger. *Mark 10:14*
Jesus experienced being tired. *John 4:6*
Jesus wept. *John 11:35*

The Bible addresses emotions:

Joy of the Lord is my strength. *Nehemiah 8:10*
A cheerful heart is good medicine. *Proverbs 17:22*
Fools vent their anger. *Proverbs 29:11*
Don't sin in your anger. *Ephesians 4:26-27*

You can choose how you manage emotions

Unhelpful ways to manage emotions:

Avoid
Deny
Shutdown
Act impulsively or reactively
Attack
Blame
Become hopeless
Take a victim role
Others: ________

Helpful ways to manage emotions:

Be curious and compassionate
Identify and name the emotion
Gain awareness
Acknowledge the truth of the emotion
Give yourself time and space
Use self-control
Manage/regulate
Others: ________

How do you typically manage your emotions?

How do you want God to help you manage your emotions?

Practical ways to manage your emotions: Touch something that calms you (pet, blanket, fidget), look at something beautiful, listen to pleasant sounds/happy song, smell something that brings you pleasure, eat or drink something that you enjoy.

Thriving Emotions

Use the Feeling Wheel to identify and explore your emotions. Expand your ability to name and understand your emotions more specifically.

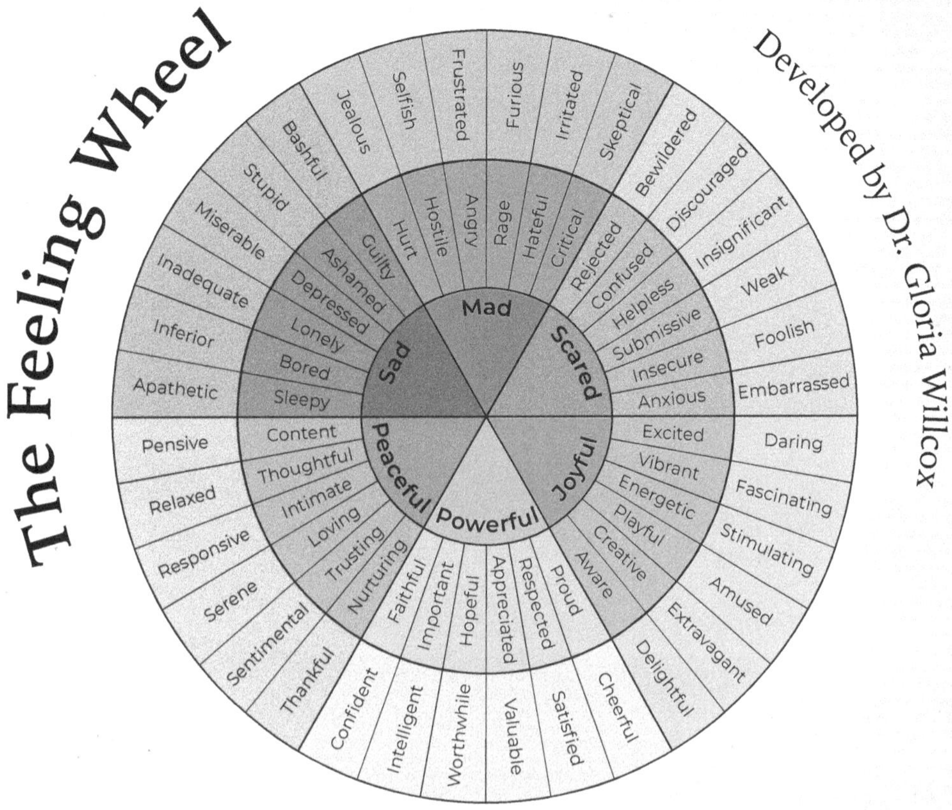

List emotions here that you regularly experience:

His peace and love dwells within you. Your default setting is peace and love.
John 14:27, 1 John 4:16-17

Emotions

Are part of your soul, basic and universal
Are hardwired into you and have a purpose
Can have many at once
Are not bad
Do not make you weak

Create rapid body arousal (survival value)
Cause you to move and act
Can be conflicting ("bittersweet")
Are sources of information for you to investigate
Can range in intensity (high, medium, low)

Action Plan : Continue to search the Scriptures for examples of how emotions are demonstrated, communicated, and experienced.

Thriving Emotions in the Bible

Throughout the Bible, both in the Old and New Testament, there are people who experience and navigate emotions in powerful ways.

David was a man after God's own heart. He experienced many emotions. Read *Psalms 17, 27, and 31.*

Write down all the emotions David documented and any emotions you experience when reading it.

You are connected to others and your emotions are visible to them. Jesus, his disciples, and those around him in the Garden of Gethsemane showed emotions. Read *Matthew 26:36-46, Mark 14:32-42, Luke 22:39-46.*

Write down all the emotions people in these passages are encountering in this situation and any emotions you experience when reading it.

Action Plan : Look in the Bible for verses that address your emotions or emotional needs. Recognize when you are experiencing strong emotions, pause, use the Power of STIL, and do the new way.

Effortlessly Change Your Emotions

When you are experiencing strong emotions, invite God into your area of need. Walk through the steps in the worksheet below to help restore you to peace with your emotions. Embrace God's Word as Him speaking to you. Accept the love God has for you. Trust in the grace, forgiveness, and mercy of Jesus Christ. Seek the counsel and comfort of the Holy Spirit. If you fully surrender to God, He will transform you from the inside out. This is effortless change.

REST: *(Matthew 11:28-30)*
Pause and be still. Breathe. Invite God into the situation.
Stay here until you can respond and not react.

What is the situation?

RECOGNIZE *(Psalm 139:23-24)*
Become aware of your emotions. Be kind to yourself in this reflection. Approach yourself and the situation with honesty, compassion, curiosity, courage, grace, and forgiveness.

What emotions are you experiencing?

RENEW *(Romans 12:2)*
Ask God what you need right now to heal, renew, and transform your emotions.
Use the Bible, Prayer, and (if helpful) the Power of STIL.

What Biblical and practical wisdom is God revealing to you?
What are your choices?

RESTORE *(Isaiah 40:31)*
Believe, receive, and act on what you have learned from God and His Word.
Honor God while you respect and love yourself and others.

Now that you have rested, recognized, and renewed, how do you want to Biblically and practically move forward to live a more Spirit-led life?

"Each time he said, 'My grace is all you need. My power works best in weakness.' So now I am glad to boast about my weaknesses, so that the power of Christ can work through me."
2 Corinthians 12:9

Thriving Words

"Don't use foul or abusive language. Let everything you say be good and helpful, so that your words will be an encouragement to those who hear them."
Ephesians 4:29

What does God say about your words?

Words have tremendous power. God spoke and all of creation came into being *(Hebrews 11:3)*. Humans are the only creatures on earth that have been given the gift of speech from God. Your words have the power to hurt or help yourself and others *(Proverbs 12:6, 18:21)*. The words you speak flow from your heart *(Matthew 12:34-35)*. Let the words of your mouth and the meditation of your heart be pleasing to God *(Psalm 19:14)*.The words of Jesus were so filled with grace that many were amazed *(Luke 4:22)*. You are created in His image and can follow His example. Speak words seasoned with grace, love, truth, and hope. How you speak is so important to God that He says you will give an account of your words one day *(Matthew 12:36-37)*. May He say to you, "Well done, good and faithful servant" *(Matthew 25:23)*.

You can choose your words

Unhelpful Words	**Helpful Words**
Manipulative	Kind, encouraging, filled with love
Mean	Build others up
Defensive	Honest
Nagging	Ask for and offer forgiveness
Lecturing	Genuine, respectful, and empathetic
Yelling	Self-controlled
Swearing	Provide sound advice
Blaming	Gentle
Gossiping	Well-thought out
Lying	Say what you mean and mean what you say
Prideful or boastful	Compassionately correct or teach

What words do you struggle with that are unhelpful?

What words can you use that are helpful?

What words do you want God to help you change? How do you want to speak instead?

Practical ways to manage words: Take a deep breath, actively listen, and think before you speak.

Action Plan: Look in the Bible for verses that address your words. Recognize when you are speaking in an unhelpful way. Pause, use the Power of STIL, and do the new way.

Effortlessly Change Your Words

Recognize when you are using unhelpful words and tone, invite God into your area of need. Walk through the steps in the worksheet below to help restore your words and tone. Embrace God's Word as Him speaking to you. Accept the love God has for you. Trust in the grace, forgiveness, and mercy of Jesus Christ. Seek the counsel and comfort of the Holy Spirit. If you fully surrender to God, He will transform you from the inside out. This is effortless change.

REST: *(Matthew 11:28-30)*
Pause and be still. Breathe. Invite God into the situation.
Stay here until you can respond and not react.

What is the situation?

RECOGNIZE *(Psalm 139:23-24)*
Become aware of your words and tone. Be kind to yourself in this reflection. Approach yourself and the situation with honesty, compassion, curiosity, courage, grace, and forgiveness.

How are you speaking (words and tone)?

RENEW *(Romans 12:2)*
Ask God what you need right now to heal, renew, and transform your words and tone.
Use the Bible, Prayer, and (if helpful) the Power of STIL.

**What Biblical and practical wisdom is God revealing to you?
What are your choices?**

RESTORE *(Isaiah 40:31)*
Believe, receive, and act on what you have learned from God and His Word.
Honor God while you respect and love yourself and others.

Now that you have rested, recognized, and renewed, how do you want to Biblically and practically move forward to live a more Spirit-led life?

"Each time he said, 'My grace is all you need. My power works best in weakness.' So now I am glad to boast about my weaknesses, so that the power of Christ can work through me."
2 Corinthians 12:9

Thriving Behaviors

"But the Holy Spirit produces this kind of fruit in our lives: love, joy, peace, patience, kindness, goodness, faithfulness, gentleness, and self-control. There is no law against these things!"
Galatians 5:22-23

What does God say about your behavior?

God empowers you to behave in a way that glories Him and benefits you and others *(Matthew 5:16)*. God has given you the power to overcome behavior that misses the mark (sin) through Christ, as well as the gift of the Holy Spirit to help you live a productive life *(Galatians 5:24-25)*. Every day, you are being transformed and renewed in His image through His grace *(2 Corinthians 3:18)*. When you misstep, and you will, be honest with God and confess your wrong doings and mistakes. Move forward knowing you are completely forgiven, accepted, and loved by God and can start again *(1 John 1:9, 2:1)*. There is no condemnation for those in Christ *(Romans 1:7)*.

Behaviors are:

Non-verbal communication shares a wealth of information. It is thought that around 70 to 95 percent of communication is non-verbal. Your facial expressions, the way you make eye contact, your posture, gestures, movement, and the way you appear in the world give others information. In addition, the tone and pitch of your voice, activity you engage in, and reactions help people understand you.

You can choose your behaviors

Unhelpful Behaviors

Disrespect
Threatening, destructive, harmful
Controlling
Pouting
Unloving
People-pleasing
Selfish
Jealousy
Division/dissension
Quarreling, scowling, rolling eyes

Helpful Behaviors

Take responsibility
Calm/use self-control
Generous
Servant-hearted
Smiley and friendly
Make appropriate eye contact
Appear engaged and interested
Demonstrate a good work ethic
Demonstrate kindness/patience
Make repairs/amends

What behaviors do you struggle with that are unhelpful?

What other behaviors can you add that are helpful to you?

Practical ways to manage your behavior:
Take a deep breath, take a moment to yourself, think before you act.

Action Plan: Look in the Bible for verses that address your behavior. Recognize when you are behaving in an unhelpful way. Pause, use the power of STIL, and do the new way.

Effortlessly Change Your Behaviors

Recognize when you are behaving in an unhelpful way, invite God into your area of need. Walk through the steps in the worksheet below to help restore your behaviors. Embrace God's Word as Him speaking to you. Accept the love God has for you. Trust in the grace, forgiveness, and mercy of Jesus Christ. Seek the counsel and comfort of the Holy Spirit. If you fully surrender to God, He will transform you from the inside out. This is effortless change.

REST: *(Matthew 11:28-30)*
Pause and be still. Breathe. Invite God into the situation.
Stay here until you can respond and not react.

What is the situation?

RECOGNIZE *(Psalm 139:23-24)*
Become aware of your behavior. Be kind to yourself in this reflection. Approach yourself and the situation with honesty, compassion, curiosity, courage, grace, and forgiveness.

How are you behaving (body language, facial expression, etc.)?

RENEW *(Romans 12:2)*
Ask God what you need right now to heal, renew, and transform your behavior.
Use the Bible, Prayer, and (if helpful) the Power of STIL.

What Biblical and practical wisdom is God revealing to you?
What are your choices?

RESTORE *(Isaiah 40:31)*
Believe, receive, and act on what you have learned from God and His Word.
Honor God while you respect and love yourself and others.

Now that you have rested, recognized, and renewed, how do you want to Biblically and practically move forward to live a more Spirit-led life?

"Each time he said, 'My grace is all you need. My power works best in weakness.' So now I am glad to boast about my weaknesses, so that the power of Christ can work through me."
2 Corinthians 12:9

The Power Of STIL: SEARCH

"Search me, O God, and know my heart; test me and know my anxious thoughts. Point out anything in me that offends you, and lead me along the path of everlasting life."
Psalm 139: 23-24

1. Get comfortable and quiet, even if for a moment (*Psalm 46:10a*).
2. Ask God to search your heart and show you areas of your life that need His touch. Anything that needs to be changed, be turned over to Him, or forgiven. For example, any emotional wounds, memories, losses, or worries that need to be healed and restored (*Psalm 139:23-24*).
3. God already knows your entire story. Because of your relationship with Jesus Christ, you can hand Him anything. He forgives you, accepts you, loves you, heals your pain, and wants the best for you (*John 3:16, 10:10; Romans 5:17*).
4. As things come up, hand them each over to the Lord and feel His loving presence filling you (*1 Peter 5:7*). Know that Jesus heals, restores, sets you free, and gives you peace (*Psalm 147:3, Mark 5:34*).
5. When you are ready, continue on with your day and do the next best thing that comes to mind that aligns with God's truth (*Philippians 1:6; 2:13*).

Now that you have practiced the Power of STIL: Search, describe your experience.

List all of things God showed you during your search. How can you use God's Word, prayer and practical steps to find healing and restoration?

The Power Of STIL: CONFESSION AND FORGIVENESS

"But if we confess our sins to Him, He is faithful and just to
forgive us our sins and to cleanse us from all wickedness."
1 John 1:9

1. Get comfortable and quiet, even if for a moment (*Psalm 46:10a*).
2. Humbly see yourself in the presence of a Holy God who loves you *(Hebrews 4:16)*. Know that every human being sins (misses the mark) and falls short of the glory of God (*Romans 3:23*). Jesus came to save the world *(John 3:16-17)* and whoever believes in Him will be completely forgiven for their sins: past, present, and future (*Hebrew 8:12*). You can boldly approach your Holy God and receive His mercy and grace *(Hebrew 4:16)*. There is now no condemnation in Christ *(Romans 8:1)*.
3. Allow Him to search your heart and show you any ways you have missed the mark (sinned) (*2 Chronicles 7:14, Psalm 139:23-24*).
4. As these wrong doings (sin) come to mind, confess them and repent (experience regret and change your way). Lay all of your sins at the foot of the cross *(1 Peter 2:24, 1 John 1:9)*.

6. Receive His love and forgiveness *(Ephesians 1:7-8, 1 John 2:2)*. Leave the sin behind for good, and move forward.
7. When you are ready, continue on with your day and do the next best thing that comes to mind that aligns with God's truth (*Philippians 1:6; 2:13*).

**Now that you have practiced the Power of STIL:
Confession and Forgiveness, describe your experience.**

**Now that God has revealed your sin and you have received His forgiveness,
what will you do differently or how will you make amends if applicable?**

**Psalm 103:12 states that God has removed your sin as far as the
East is from the West. Describe what this means to you. Look up additional
verses in the Bible that describe the fullness of God's forgiveness.**

Effortlessly Change Your Situation

Recognize when you are experiencing a challenging situation, your soul is overwhelmed, and your body is reacting. Walk through all areas of your soul and body to restore your thoughts, emotions, words, and behaviors. Invite God into your areas of need. Embrace God's Word as Him speaking to you. Accept the love God has for you. Trust in the grace, forgiveness, and mercy of Jesus Christ. Seek the counsel and comfort of the Holy Spirit. If you fully surrender to God, He will transform you from the inside out. This is effortless change.

REST *(Matthew 11:28-30)*
Pause and be still. Breathe. Invite God into the situation.
Stay here until you can respond and not react.

What is the situation?

RECOGNIZE *(Psalm 139:23-24)*
Become aware of your **thoughts, emotions, words, and behaviors**. Be kind to yourself in this reflection. Approach yourself and the situation with honesty, compassion, curiosity, courage, grace, and forgiveness.

What thoughts, emotions, words, and behaviors are you experiencing?

RENEW *(Romans 12:2)*
Ask God what you need right now to heal, renew, and transform your **thoughts, emotions, words, and behaviors**. Use the Bible, Prayer, and (if helpful) the Power of STIL.

What Biblical and practical wisdom is God revealing to you?
What are your choices?

RESTORE *(Isaiah 40:31)*
Believe, receive, and act on what you have learned from God and His Word.
Honor God while you respect and love yourself and others.

Now that you have rested, recognized, and renewed, how do you want to Biblically and practically move forward to live a more Spirit-led life?

Effortless Change

Rest

Recognize

Renew

Restore

"Each time he said, "My grace is all you need. My power works best in weakness." So now I am glad to boast about my weaknesses, so that the power of Christ can work through me."

2 Corinthians 12:9

Journal

Take a moment to reflect on what you have learned about yourself and God.

Explore God's Word

Take the time to read each of these verses about Thriving Inside And Out.

"Study this Book of Instruction continually. Meditate on it day and night so you will be sure to obey everything written in it. Only then will you prosper and succeed in all you do."
Joshua 1:8

"And so, dear brothers and sisters, I plead with you to give your bodies to God because of all he has done for you. Let them be a living and holy sacrifice—the kind he will find acceptable. This is truly the way to worship him. Don't copy the behavior and customs of this world, but let God transform you into a new person by changing the way you think. Then you will learn to know God's will for you, which is good and pleasing and perfect."
Romans 12:1-3

"Love is patient and kind. Love is not jealous or boastful or proud or rude. It does not demand its own way. It is not irritable, and it keeps no record of being wronged. It does not rejoice about injustice but rejoices whenever the truth wins out. Love never gives up, never loses faith, is always hopeful, and endures through every circumstance."
1 Corinthians 13:4-7

"We destroy every proud obstacle that keeps people from knowing God. We capture their rebellious thoughts and teach them to obey Christ."
2 Corinthians 10:5

"So let's not get tired of doing what is good. At just the right time we will reap a harvest of blessing if we don't give up."
Galatians 6:9

"Throw off your old sinful nature and your former way of life, which is corrupted by lust and deception. Instead, let the Spirit renew your thoughts and attitudes. Put on your new nature, created to be like God—truly righteous and holy."
Ephesians 4:22-24

"Dear brothers and sisters, when troubles of any kind come your way, consider it an opportunity for great joy. For you know that when your faith is tested, your endurance has a chance to grow. So let it grow, for when your endurance is fully developed, you will be perfect and complete, needing nothing."
James 1:2-4

"And I will forgive their wickedness, and I will never again remember their sins."
Hebrews 8:12

Scan the code with your mobile device for a prayer.

Core Truth 5:

COME TO THE TABLE

"My command is this: Love each other as I have loved you.
Greater love has no one than this: to
lay down one's life for one's friends."
John 15:12-13

WELCOME

to

COME TO THE TABLE

The purpose of Come To The Table is to help you recognize, prioritize, and pray for people in your life.

Scan the code with your mobile device for a video introducing Come To The Table

THE MAP: GOD'S WORD

God says in His Word you were created to be in contact with Him and to put Him and His priorities first *(Exodus 20:1-17, Matthew 6:33)*. You'll be more successful in all areas of your life if you have an intimate connection with God.

He also said that it is not good for you to be alone. He created others on this earth with the intention that you would form relationships and a sense of connectedness and belonging with them *(Genesis 2:18)*. God uses His people that are placed in your life to encourage, support, educate, assist, defend, compassionately correct, protect, and pray for you; they also want and need the same in return *(Ecclesiastes 4:9-12, Matthew 18:19-20)*. God is clear that He wants you to lead your life with love because He is love, He loved you first and wants you to love others as you do yourself *(Matthew 22:37-39; John 4:7-20, 15:12-13)*.

PRACTICAL STEPS FOR YOUR JOURNEY

THOUGHTS FOR THE JOURNEY:

Invite God to be at your table. He wants to be an integral part of the relationships that surround your table.

Think about who really matters and is a part of your life. Focus on giving them the best version of you. Be audaciously generous with your time, talents, and resources.

You have impact on others and vice versa. Be aware of how you influence others.

Every aspect of your life, from how you approach others and interact with them, can be a reflection of the love of God and being Jesus-like (Ephesians 5:1-2).

The people at your table may vary in age, diversity, strengths, values, personality, geography, and so much more. Embrace those that are around you.

ACTIONS FOR THE JOURNEY:

- Be open to allowing new people to your table and growing a welcoming table.
- Be more concerned with loving people rather than your agenda or specific outcomes.
- Have realistic expectations and meet individuals where they are.
- Remember we are all works in progress. Be gracious and merciful.
- Join groups and activities that pique your interest. Be inquisitive, teachable, and open-minded.
- Make creative efforts to interact with others in new ways.
- Be willing to ask for and to offer support.
- When possible, put down your devices and visit in person with people.
- Create a list of people at your table, and start praying for their needs
- If you are feeling lonely, isolated, or desiring greater connection with others:
  * Remember God is always with you and He loves you.
  * Pray for God to expand your table with meaningful relationships.
  * Keep working on building a Christ-centered healthy self-concept (Core Truth 3).
  * If you struggle with social skills, consider books, counseling, and/or coaching to improve your skills.
  * Be courageous and creative in finding opportunities to meet new people that share your interests (book club, church Bible Study, volunteer, arts, sports, attend a community education event, etc.).

ROADBLOCKS COMMON TO THE JOURNEY:

Shyness	Close-minded	Over-functioning
Pride	Insecurity	(over-involved/too busy)
Selfishness	Inferiority	Under-functioning
Unforgiveness	Perfectionism	(isolated/lonely)
Bitterness/Anger	People-pleasing	Fear
Lacking in social skills	Unhealthy boundaries	

When you identify a roadblock, call on God to help you overcome that roadblock and choose a new path. Know that Jesus has come to set you free (John 8:36). It is possible to overcome!

THE PATH: WORKBOOK ACTIVITIES

Turn to page 69, "Table of Connection," read through and follow the instructions to build your invitation list for your personal table.

Turn to page 70, "Reflections on your Community," to help you become aware of the people and the connections you have.

Turn to page 71, "The Power of STIL: Praise and Worship," and "The Power of STIL: Prayer," follow the instructions and spend time with God.

Turn to page 72, "Journal," and share things you have learned and things you want to change or maintain.

Turn to page 73, "Explore God's Word," to deepen your walk with God.

Table Of Connection

Who has God placed around you?
Ecclesiastes 4:9-12

Write in all the people God has placed at your table (spouse, children, neighbor, parent, grandparents, extended family members, co-workers, friends, people at church, etc.). Seat people in the order of closeness to you. For example, you may want to have your parent, spouse, or child next to you and people at church further out on the table or at a different table based on your closeness to them.

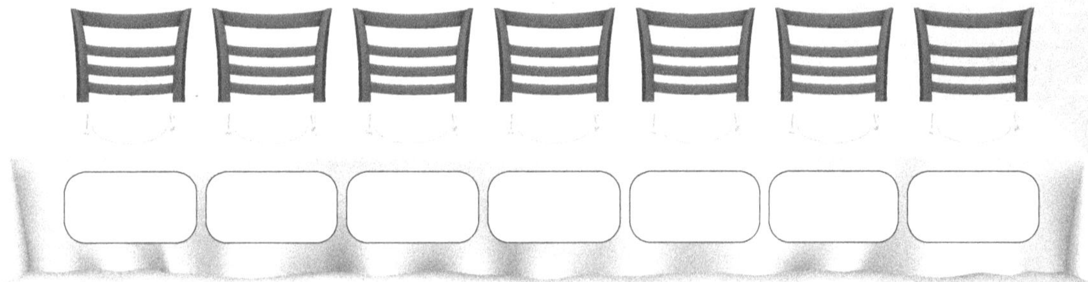

You have people at your Table of Connection. Some reasons for connection are: to encourage, learn, play, grow, love, support, challenge and help.

What are some other reasons you want and need connection?

Action Plan: Look in the Bible for ways God connected people to each other (disciples, spouses, siblings, etc).

Reflections On Your Community

Write a list of people for whom to pray and their needs.
James 5:16

Is God placing anyone on your heart that you need to forgive?
Ephesians 4:32

How can you connect to the people in your world so you add value to their lives?

Who can you ask to pray for you, and what are your needs?

What are the strengths of the people at your table, and how have they blessed you?

The Power Of STIL: PRAISE AND WORSHIP

"Let everything that breathes sing praises to the LORD!"
Psalm 150:6

1. Start singing, speaking your love and adoration for God (*Psalm 100:4-5, Ephesians 5:19*).
2. Be yourself and just enjoy your time rejoicing with your Lord (*Philippians 4:4*).

The Power Of STIL: PRAYER

"Always be joyful. Never stop praying. Be thankful in all circumstances, for this is God's will for you who belong to Christ Jesus."
1 Thessalonians 5:16-18

1. Get comfortable and quiet, even if for a moment (*Psalm 46:10a*).
2. Embrace the holy presence of the Lord (*Isaiah 6:1-4, Habakkuk 2:20*).
3. Imagine God present with you. Approach Him with a heart of respect, expectation, praise, and gratitude (*Psalm 100:4-5*).
3. Know that God loves you and wants a relationship with you. Talk to Him. Tell Him the truth about everything. He cares for you, He is listening, and He wants to help you (*Psalm 32:8, Isaiah 43:2*).
4. Stay present and real with God. Feel free to cry, laugh, sit quietly, dance, or walk. Pour out your heart to Him (your needs, others' needs, circumstances, etc.). Allow yourself to let go and be with your Father God.
5. Know that your prayers have power. Expect they will be answered in God's perfect way and timing (*Matthew 21:22, Mark 11:24, John 14:13-14*).
6. When you are ready, continue on with your day and do the next best thing that comes to mind that aligns with God's truth (*Philippians 1:6; 2:13*).

Now that you have practiced the Power of STIL: Praise and Worship and Prayer, describe your experience.

Action Plan: Create a plan for daily practice of praise and prayer.

Journal

Reflect on your table. What can you do to connect more fully with people at your table? What can you do to build new relationships? How can you create more meaningful connections in your life?

Explore God's Word

Take the time to read each of these verses about Come To The Table.

"Then the Lord God said,
'It is not good for the man to be alone.
I will make a helper who is just right for him.'"
Genesis 2:18

"Two people are better off than one, for they can help each other succeed. If one person falls, the other can reach out and help. But someone who falls alone is in real trouble. Likewise, two people lying close together can keep each other warm. But how can one be warm alone? A person standing alone can be attacked and defeated, but two can stand back-to-back and conquer. Three are even better, for a triple-braided cord is not easily broken."
Ecclesiastes 4:9-12

"I also tell you this: If two of you agree here on earth concerning anything you ask, my Father in heaven will do it for you. For where two or three gather together as my followers, I am there among them."
Matthew 18:19-20

"And he called his twelve disciples together and began sending them out two by two, giving them authority to cast out evil spirits."
Mark 6:7

This is my commandment: Love each other in the same way I have loved you. There is no greater love than to lay down one's life for one's friends.
John 15:12-13

Paul was alone and disconnected from people and waiting to be executed.
He was asking for his people to come see him. Reach out and ask for help.
"As for me, my life has already been poured out as an offering to God.
The time of my death is near...
Timothy, please come as soon as you can...
Only Luke is with me. Bring Mark with you when you come,
for he will be helpful to me in my ministry.
The first time I was brought before the judge, no one came with me.
Everyone abandoned me. May it not be counted against them...
Do your best to get here before winter. Eubulus sends you greetings,
and so do Pudens, Linus, Claudia, and all the brothers and sisters."
2 Timothy 4:6, 9, 11, 16, 21

Scan the code with your mobile device for a prayer.

Core Truth 6:

STAND FIRM

"Be on your guard; stand firm in the faith, be courageous; be strong. Do everything in love."

1 Corinthians 16:13-14

WELCOME

to

STAND FIRM

The purpose of Stand Firm is to help you become aware of and apply healthy Biblical boundaries for yourself and others.

Scan the code with your mobile device for a video introducing Stand Firm

THE MAP: GOD'S WORD

God says in His Word that He is not a God of disorder but one of peace *(1 Corinthians 14:33)*. He set limits for your benefit, and His Scriptures have a solution for everything in your life *(2 Timothy 3:16-17)*. God uses the principle of reaping and sowing to teach you what your life will yield *(Galatians 6:7-10)*. He also knows that boundaries are difficult to implement. Through Jesus, He continually gives you grace, mercy, and forgiveness on this journey.

God wants you to pursue the path of wisdom *(Proverbs 4:6-7)*. The more you learn God's Word, the more it will transform you. When you put God's Word into practice, the greater your success *(Joshua 1:8)*. The Bible and prayer can assist you in determining which path to follow in life *(Proverbs 3:5-6, Philippians 4:6-7)*. For example, the Bible says good boundaries protect you from negative consequences, keep you safe, correct you, require you to be honest, help you take responsibility for your actions, navigate relationships, communicate, manage your money and so on *(Deuteronomy 8:18, Proverbs 22:24, Ephesians 4:25, 32; James 1:19, 1 Peter 2:17)*. His Word clearly says that God will instruct you on which way to go *(Psalm 32:8, Isaiah 30:21)*.

PRACTICAL STEPS FOR YOUR JOURNEY

THOUGHTS FOR THE JOURNEY:

God wants you to have healthy limits in all areas of your life. The following are some of the major boundaries: Physical (land and water); Spiritual (the Ten Commandments); Personal (how you manage your money, clothes you wear); Relational (honor your mother and father, treat each other with respect); and Societal (laws and rules, such as wear your seat belt, do not steal).

Boundaries are limits that are not to be crossed without permission. They separate one thing from another. They help you define what is important and what is unimportant. They help you define who you are and who you are not, what you will do and what you will not.

Go to the Word of God for any area in your life where you are having difficulty, and see what God has to say about it. Be a God-pleaser, not a man-pleaser *(Acts 5:29, Galatians 1:10)*.

ACTIONS FOR THE JOURNEY:

- Standing firm in your faith during trials develops endurance, character, hope *(Romans 5:3-5)*.
- Let your "yes" be "yes" and your "no" be "no" *(Matthew 5:37)*. Know who you are and your core values. Respectfully and clearly communicate them to others.
- Respect and honor the differences in yourself and others.
- Do not enable harmful or sinful behaviors of others.
- Be aware when you find yourself in a position where you are overworked, over-extended, mistreated, and under appreciated. Speak up in love and re-establish your boundaries.
- Be aware when you are crossing others boundaries.
- Respectfully and calmly let someone know when they have hurt you or crossed the line with you. Confront people in love, be willing to forgive, and re-establish the boundary with clarity.
- Have clear expectations of yourself and others. Seek clarification when there is miscommunication.

ROADBLOCKS COMMON TO THE JOURNEY:

Mind reading	Under-functioning	Perfectionism
Assuming	Reactive	Rescuing
People-pleasing	Being too passive	Fixing
Over-functioning	Being too aggressive	Care-taking

When you identify a roadblock, call on God to help you overcome that roadblock and choose a new path. Know that Jesus has come to set you free (John 8:36). It is possible to overcome!

THE PATH: WORKBOOK ACTIVITIES

Turn to page 77, "What Are Boundaries," to learn the definition of boundaries and bring clarity that God created boundaries and wants you to implement His Word for practical daily living.

Turn to page 78, "Sow and Reap Well," to learn to recognize how your thoughts and actions have consequences. What you plant you will harvest in your life. Read through the list of helpful and unhelpful boundaries to explore your own boundaries.

Turn to page 79, "Consequences, Grace, and Forgiveness," to understand that God's compassionate correction (discipline) is always good for you and designed to bring peace, right living, and set you on course for His purpose.

Turn to pages 80-82, "Helpful Biblical Boundaries" for examples of boundaries God wants you to honor and obey and to learn how to express your own boundaries in helpful ways.

Turn to page 83, "Effortlessly Change Your Boundaries" read and follow the instructions to learn and practice thriving in your boundaries.

Turn to page 84, "Journal" and share things you have learned and things you want to change or maintain.

Turn to page 85, "Explore God's Word" to deepen your walk with God.

What Are Boundaries?

"Then God said, 'Let there be a space between the waters, to separate the waters of the heavens from the waters of the earth.'"
Genesis 1:6

What does God say about boundaries?

From the beginning God designed His creation with boundaries. They are created to bring order and personally keep everyones spirit, soul and body safe. Boundaries can be generically defined as lines/borders between people, places and things. They let you know where one thing ends and another begins. God has specific boundaries in Scripture. He knows that boundaries are difficult to implement. Through Jesus, He continually gives you grace, mercy, and forgiveness on this journey.

God designed creation and you to have boundaries.
God is a God of order and not a God of chaos.

God designed boundaries for your benefit.
Go to His Word. He has an answer for every area of your life.
2 Timothy 3:16-17

- How you are to live
- How you are to love
- How you are to work and study
- How you are to manage our money
- How you parent
- How you live out our marriage
- How you treat each other
- How you take care of yourself
- How you think, feel, speak, behave
- How you are a good neighbor/friend

Boundaries are limits/borders.
God calls you to be imitators of Him.
Ephesians 5:1-2

- A line that separates one thing from another
- They help you define what you value and what you don't
- Who you are and who you are not
- What you believe and what you don't
- What you accept and what you don't
- What you will give and what you won't

When you think of boundaries, what comes to mind?

Sow and Reap Well

"Don't be misled—you cannot mock the justice of God. You will always harvest what you plant. Those who live only to satisfy their own sinful nature will harvest decay and death from that sinful nature. But those who live to please the Spirit will harvest everlasting life from the Spirit. So let's not get tired of doing what is good. At just the right time we will reap a harvest of blessing if we don't give up. Therefore, whenever we have the opportunity, we should do good to everyone—especially to those in the family of faith."
Galatians 6:7-10

What does God say about sowing and reaping?

In the Scripture above, God gives you a clear example that your thoughts and actions (sowing) have consequences (reaping). To demonstrate boundaries, He shares the principle of sowing and reaping and calls you to live a Spirit-led life. He uses a farming example of planting a field to show that what you plant and grow, you will harvest. For example, when you plant anger and grow anger, you experience more anger. When you plant joy and grow joy, you experience more joy.

You can choose your boundaries

Unhelpful boundaries	**Helpful boundaries**
Reactive	Loving and respectful of others
Dominating/controlling	Consistent and clear
Passive/aggressive	Firm and flexible
Under-functioning	Assertiveness
Over-functioning	Respectful
Irresponsible	Honoring commitments
Inflexible/rigid	Responsible
People-pleasing	Your "Yes" is "Yes"
Enabling	Your "No" is "No"
Rescuing/fixing	Honest

What boundaries do you struggle with that are unhelpful?

What other behaviors can you add that are helpful to you?

How would you like to change a boundary so that you sow and reap better?

Consequences, Grace, and Forgiveness

For our earthly fathers disciplined us for a few years, doing the best they knew how. But God's discipline is always good for us, so that we might share in his holiness. No discipline is enjoyable while it is happening—it's painful! But afterward there will be a peaceful harvest of right living for those who are trained in this way.
Hebrews 12:10-11

What does God say about consequences, grace and forgiveness?

Your Heavenly Father's compassionate correction (discipline) is never to bring punishment, shame, or condemnation upon you when you cross boundaries or miss the mark *(Romans 8:1)*. Jesus has completely taken away all your sin, shame, and punishment through the cross *(I Thessalonians 5:9)*. However, in this life our actions create consequences. God's Word says His discipline is always good for you. It brings peace into your life, corrects you to right living aligned with His Word, and sets you on course for His purpose. God's spiritual principles are based on love for you and done with a heart of nurturing, encouragement, freedom, and healing. They are designed for your good and not to harm you. They convict, restore, transform, provide a way out, and grant you greater wisdom *(1 Corinthians 10:13, James 1:5)*. God's teachings bring freedom and liberation through the finished work of Jesus Christ *(John 8:36)*.

As you move forward, recognize when you have crossed your or someone else's boundaries or make a misstep. Immediately confess when you miss the mark (sin). Receive His love, grace, and forgiveness *(Ephesians 1:7-8, 1 John 2:2)*. Know that you are fully forgiven, perfectly accepted, deeply loved, and leave the past behind for good *(John 15:12-13, Romans 5:17, Hebrews 8:12)*.

Becoming more Christ-like is a life-long, daily process. His grace is sufficient *(2 Corinthians 12:9)*. Draw near to Him, and He will draw near to you *(Psalm 145:18, James 4:8)*. God saved you by grace when you believed, and you can't take credit for this; it is a gift from God. Receive this gift and undeserved favor from your God, be set free, and be transformed *(Acts 15:11,Ephesians 2:8, Romans 5:20)*. Extend this same forgiveness, grace, and mercy to others *(Ephesians 4:32)*.

How have boundaries and consequences helped you learn, grow, and understand God's grace and forgiveness?

Helpful Biblical Boundaries

Below are examples of helpful Biblical boundaries.

Protect yourself from negative consequences
"...they will eat the fruit of their ways and be filled with the fruit of their schemes."
Proverbs 1:31

Choose your friends wisely
"Do not make friends with a hot-tempered person, do not associate with one easily angered."
Proverbs 22:24

Accept correction when given and offer correction when needed
"Whoever rebukes a person will in the end gain favor
rather than one who has a flattering tongue."
Proverbs 28:23

Let your "Yes" be "Yes" and your "No" be "No" without guilt or overly justifying your reasons
"Just say a simple, 'Yes, I will,' or 'No, I won't.' Anything beyond this is from the evil one."
Matthew 5:37

Put limits on unhelpful relationships
"Don't be fooled by those who say such things, for 'bad company corrupts good character.'"
1 Corinthians 15:33

Be honest
"So stop telling lies. Let us tell our neighbors the truth, for we are all parts of the same body."
Ephesians 4:25

Take personal responsibility for your own behavior and offer forgiveness
"Instead, be kind to each other, tenderhearted, forgiving one another,
just as God through Christ has forgiven you."
Ephesians 4:32

Listen to one another and consider your own communication
"Understand this, my dear brothers and sisters:
You must all be quick to listen, slow to speak, and slow to get angry."
James 1:19

Treat one another with respect and love
"Remember, it is better to suffer for doing good, if that is what God wants,
than to suffer for doing wrong!"
1 Peter 2:7

Helpful Biblical Boundaries

Everyone, from time to time, struggles with boundaries, which can have internal and external consequences. Read the following three stories and write about the boundaries that were crossed, the resulting internal and external consequences, and God's grace.

Read *Genesis 12:1-20* about the story of Abraham and explore his relationship with God, his lies, his relationships with his wife and others, his cross-cultural experiences, consequences of sin, and God's grace.

Read 2 *Samuel Chapters 11-12* about the story of David, his position, his power, his choices, his relationships, his repentance, and his restoration.

Read the story in *Romans Chapters 7-8* of Paul and his struggle with sin and living through the grace of Jesus.

Expressing Biblical Boundaries

Expressing your Biblical Boundaries requires you to look upward (to God through prayer and His Word), inward (check for your weaknesses based on Matthew 7:4-5, know your strengths and what you clearly want to share) and outward (the person you are going to talk to is also God's creation therefore, has value and worth).

Effective communication includes being the following:

Calm	Loving, kind, gracious, and forgiving
Humble	Interested in understanding the other person's viewpoint
Respectful	Slow (kind tone and easy tempo)
Open-minded	Simple (clear and concise)
Quick to listen	Soft (gentle yet firm)
Slow to speak	Polite and with invitation shares perspective
Slow to anger	Verifies understanding of the other person's viewpoint
Affirming	Respectful and embraces others differences
Collaborative	Honorable and does what is agreed upon.

Expressing Biblical Boundaries

One way to discover and express your Biblical Boundary is by stating to yourself or others the following:

"It's okay ________(helpful boundary), it's not okay ________(unhelpful boundary)."

For example: "It's okay to disagree with me and be mad; it's not okay to swear or yell."

Another way to begin expressing your Biblical Boundary is to use a statement such as:

" I feel ________(state your emotion)
about ________(state the fact of the situation; discuss the problem not the person).
I want, desire, or hope for the following ________(state or ask for your desired outcome)."
Now ask for their buy in or willingness to work together. Recognize everyone has a choice and so do you. Based on their response, you get to decide what you do next.

For example: "I feel frustrated and overwhelmed about the way we are communicating.
I want us to speak calmly with love and kindness to each other.
Would you be willing to work with me on this?"

What helpful Biblical Boundaries do you want to improve and express to others?

Effortlessly Change Your Boundaries

Recognize when you are experiencing a situation where your boundary is being challenged, your soul is overwhelmed and your body is reacting. Walk through all areas of your soul and body to restore your thoughts, emotions, words and behaviors. Invite God into your areas of need. Embrace God's Word as Him speaking to you. Accept the love God has for you. Trust in the grace, forgiveness, and mercy of Jesus Christ. Seek the counsel and comfort of the Holy Spirit. If you fully surrender to God, He will transform you from the inside out. This is effortless change.

REST *(Matthew 11:28-30)*
Pause and be still. Breathe. Invite God into the situation.
Stay here until you can respond and not react.

What is the situation?

RECOGNIZE *(Psalm 139:23-24)*
Become aware of your **thoughts, emotions, words, and behaviors around your boundary**. Be kind to yourself in this reflection. Approach yourself and the situation with honesty, compassion, curiosity, courage, grace, and forgiveness.

What thoughts, emotions, words, and behaviors are you experiencing?

RENEW *(Romans 12:2)*
Ask God what you need right now to heal, renew, and transform your **thoughts, emotions, words, and behaviors around your boundary**. Use the Bible, Prayer, and (if helpful) the Power of STIL.

**What Biblical and practical wisdom is God revealing to you?
What are your choices?**

RESTORE *(Isaiah 40:31)*
Believe, receive, and act on what you have learned from God and His Word.
Honor God while you respect and love yourself and others.

Now that you have rested, recognized, and renewed, how do you want to Biblically and practically move forward to live a more Spirit-led life?

Journal

Take a moment to reflect on what you have learned about helpful Biblical boundaries.

Explore God's Word

Take the time to read each of these verses about Stand Firm

"And the Lord God commanded the man, 'You are free to eat from any tree in the garden; but you must not eat from the tree of the knowledge of good and evil, for when you eat from it you will certainly die.' "
Genesis 2:16-17

The Ten Commandments
Exodus 20:3-17

"Who kept the sea inside its boundaries
as it burst from the womb,
and as I clothed it with clouds
and wrapped it in thick darkness?
For I locked it behind barred gates,
limiting its shores.
I said, 'This far and no farther will you come.
Here your proud waves must stop!'"
Job 38:8-11

"Just say a simple, 'Yes, I will,' or 'No, I won't.' Anything beyond this is from the evil one."
Mathew 5:37

"For we are each responsible for our own conduct."
Galatians 6:5

"Imitate God, therefore, in everything you do, because you are his dear children. Live a life filled with love, following the example of Christ. He loved us and offered himself as a sacrifice for us, a pleasing aroma to God. Let there be no sexual immorality, impurity, or greed among you. Such sins have no place among God's people. Obscene stories, foolish talk, and coarse jokes—these are not for you. Instead, let there be thankfulness to God."
Ephesians 5:1-4

"So, my dear brothers and sisters, be strong and immovable. Always work enthusiastically for the Lord, for you know that nothing you do for the Lord is ever useless."
I Corinthians 15:58

Scan the code with your mobile device for a prayer.

Core Truth 7:

LIVE OUT LOUD

**"Do not merely listen to the Word,
and so deceive yourself, do what it says."**

James 1:22

WELCOME
to
LIVE OUT LOUD

The purpose of Live Out Loud is to assist you in formulating God-honoring goals for your daily life and building the future God has planned for you.

Scan the code with your mobile device for a video introducing Live Out Loud

THE MAP: GOD'S WORD

You are the handiwork of God, made new in Christ to do good works on earth *(Ephesians 2:10)*. God invites you to seek Him so His goals can be woven into your life and heart. He is trustworthy, reliable, and relational *(Psalms 33:11, 37:4-5, 127:1; Proverbs 3:6, 16:9)*. Writing down what He reveals to you regarding your dreams and goals will help you stay on course *(Habakkuk 2:2)*. Run your race with God and maintain your faith until you reach the finish line *(2 Timothy 4:7; Hebrews 12:1)*. You are filled with the power and might of God. He has equipped you with the strength and capacity to achieve every goal aligned with His will *(Isaiah 40:31, Philippians 4-13, Hebrews 10:35-36)*.

As a child of God, embrace His grace and live in the present *(2 Corinthians 12:9, Hebrews 11:1)*. Look forward with hope and press on in Christ *(Philippians 3:14)*. Give your worries about tomorrow and the future to God *(Matthew 6:34)*. As you begin each day, keep your gaze fixed on Him, the author and finisher of your faith *(Hebrews 12:2)*.

PRACTICAL STEPS FOR YOUR JOURNEY

THOUGHTS FOR THE JOURNEY:

God is faithful and will lead you towards His purpose *(Ephesians 2:10)*.

Your journey of life can be fun and filled with the fruit of the Spirit.

Faith is hope with expectation in the now *(Hebrews 11:1, James 4:13-14)*. Live in the present.

You are not alone on this journey. God is with you and He has placed others in your life to encourage you.

Making small consistent changes every day will lead toward transformation.

ACTIONS FOR THE JOURNEY:

- Review your vision/dream board and check if it aligns with everything you have learned about God, yourself, and others.
- Create and cultivate an attitude of contentment in the everyday journey toward your goal.
- Allow yourself time to heal from past failures and challenges, everyone has them. Use what you've learned from the past in the present.
- Make sure to include goals to rest, relax, and rejuvenate.
- Move at a pace that fits your ability and circumstance. You may have to idle, reverse, or proceed on occasion. Go slow, keep it simple, and be kind to yourself.
- Live in faith, be courageous, pray, trust God, and enjoy the journey.
- Be committed, diligent, and persevere when the going gets tough.
- Act with authority and confidence.
- Be solution-oriented and not problem-oriented.
- Align your will with God's will.

ROADBLOCKS COMMON TO THE JOURNEY:

Fear	Pride	Perfectionism
Procrastination	Distractions	Negative false beliefs about self

When you identify a roadblock, call on God to help you overcome that roadblock and choose a new path. Know that Jesus has come to set you free (John 8:36). It is possible to overcome!

THE PATH: WORKBOOK ACTIVITIES

Turn to page 89, "Live out Loud: Presence and Purpose," to wrap up the 7 Core Truths together. When activated together in faith we believe you will begin to live life out loud.

Turn to page 90, "Godly Goals are S.M.A.R.T.," read the components of Godly Goals and begin reflecting on how goals can support who you are becoming versus just setting a goal to achieve.

Turn to page 91, "Goal Sheet Action Plan," and choose one area to create S.M.A.R.T. goals using the questions to guide your design and specifics of this goals

Turn to page 92, "Daily Thriving with Purpose," for an easy format to help guide your daily life concerning all 7 Core Truths.

Turn to page 93, "The Power of STIL: Declarations," and follow the directions to learn to speak life into your dreams and goals.

Turn to page 94, "Summary Statement," to write all that you have learned and how you will move forward thriving in life.

Turn to page 95, "Explore God's Word," to deepen your walk with God.

Live Out Loud: PRESENCE AND PURPOSE

PAST:
Remember your history before coming to Christ *(Ephesians 2:11-13)*, but do not be a prisoner of it *(Luke 9:62)*. Look forward and press on with Christ (*Philippians 3:13-14*).

PRESENT:
Faith is in the now *(Hebrews 11:1, James 4:13-14)*, and His grace is all we need (2 Corinthians 12:9).

FUTURE:
Plan ahead *(Luke 14:28)*, but don't worry about the future (*Matthew 6:34*). Press on toward the heavenly prize *(Philippians 2:12-14)* and the glorious transformation that lies ahead *(Philippians 3:20-21)*.

Dare To Dream

Connect With God

Know Who You Are

Thrive Inside And Out

Come To The Table

Stand Firm

Live Out Loud

PURPOSE:
"For we are God's masterpiece. He has created us anew in Christ Jesus, so we can do the good things He planned for us long ago."
Ephesians 2:10

Action Plan: Look back at your original dream/vision and ask yourself if there is anything you would change to bring it into alignment with what you have learned.

Godly Goals Are S.M.A.R.T.

"Take delight in the Lord, and He will give you your heart's desires.
Commit everything you do to the Lord. Trust Him, and He will help you."
Psalm 37:4-5

Now that you have walked through the Core Truths, it is time to act, and write down your next steps toward living your God given purpose and desired life. There are many categories in your life on which to focus. You don't need to do them all at once. Goals are achieved through making small changes in your daily routines. Over time these actions create habits that lead to transformation.

Choose one or two areas in your life to focus on first. Use what you have learned during your time with God and your knowledge of His Word to help you create S.M.A.R.T. (Specific, Measurable, Achievable, Relevant, and Time-sensitive) Goals. They can be short-term, intermediate, or long-term. These goals are meant to start out small and be revisited often. Small changes lead to big gains. Remember to celebrate each step of success along the way.

Areas to consider for Godly Goals

God
Marriage
Family/parenting
Work
Finances
School
Living environment
Personal growth
Health/recreation
Community

Steps to Godly Goals

Seek God's will
Pray first
Go slow
Stay motivated
Have accountability partners
Celebrate successes
Create a plan for obstacles
Persevere when it gets hard

Examples:

Your Motivation(your why): I want to be a healthier person.
Health Goal: I will eat one fruit (specific/relevant) every day (measurable/achievable) for the next 3 weeks (time-sensitive).

Your Motivation(your why): I want to be closer to God.
Spiritual Goal : I will read 1-2 verses in the Bible daily and meditate on them for the next week.

What area do you want to focus on first?

Goal Sheet Action Plan

"In the same way, let your good deeds shine out for all to see,
so that everyone will praise your heavenly Father."
Matthew 5:16

What is your S.M.A.R.T. Goal?

What does God say about this goal?

What is your motivation (your why) for this goal?

What helpful qualities do you see in others who have had success with this goal?

What do you need to believe about yourself for this goal?

What obstacles might you encounter?

What are some solutions to your obstacles?

Who can you connect with today to raise your accountability for this goal?

What is the first step that can take toward making your goal a habit?

Daily Thriving With Purpose

"This is the day the Lord has made.
We will rejoice and be glad in it."
Psalm 118:24
Start your day off Living Out Loud.

How will you live connected to your dream/vision?

How will you renew your thoughts today?

How will you connect to God today?

How can you create more peace in your life today?

What is one of your values/strengths?

How can you show love and respect with your words and actions?

How can you take care of yourself today?

What people can you pray for today?

What Bible verse will you focus on today?

How will you stand firm today?

Who does Christ say you are?

What S.M.A.R.T. Goal will you focus on?

How will you care for your body today?

What Power of STIL will help you today?

The Power Of STIL: DECLARATIONS

"And we are confident that He hears us whenever
we ask for anything that pleases Him."
1 John 5:14

1. Get comfortable and quiet, even if for a moment (*Psalm 46:10a*).
2. Search the Bible, Internet, or Bible App for all the verses matching your area of need in this moment *(Roman 10:17)*. For example, if you need courage, search Scriptures for when you need courage. Take the list and write them out in the first person. For example, "You are filled with power, love, and a sound mind"*(2 Timothy 1:7)* becomes "I am filled with power, love, and a sound mind."
3. Read and re-read the Scriptures out loud. Do as often as necessary (*Joshua 1:8*).
4. Reading or speaking the Scriptures and not writing them is completely fine. Personalizing and writing them is Biblical and can be more intimate (*Genesis 1:3, John 1:1*). If you are declaring Scriptures for others, simply insert their names.
5. When you are ready, continue on with your day and do the next best thing that comes to mind that aligns with God's truth (*Philippians 1:6; 2:13*).

Now that you have practiced the Power of STIL: Declarations, describe your experience.

Summary Statement

Write a few sentences that summarize what you have learned, where you are now, and how you are going to continue to Thrive in Life.

Explore God's Word

Take the time to read each of these verses about Live Out Loud.

"This is my command—be strong and courageous! Do not be afraid or discouraged.
For the Lord your God is with you wherever you go."
Joshua 1:9

"May He give you the desire of your heart
and make all your plans succeed."
Psalm 20:4

"You are the light of the world—like a city on a hilltop that cannot be hidden. No one lights a lamp and then puts it under a basket. Instead, a lamp is placed on a stand, where it gives light to everyone in the house. In the same way, let your good deeds shine out for all to see, so that everyone will praise your heavenly Father.
Matthew 5:14-16

"Jesus came and told His disciples, "I have been given all authority in heaven and on earth. Therefore, go and make disciples of all the nations, baptizing them in the name of the Father and the Son and the Holy Spirit. Teach these new disciples to obey all the commands I have given you. And be sure of this: I am with you always, even to the end of the age."
Matthew 28:18-20

"But He said to me, 'My grace is sufficient for you, for my power is made perfect in weakness.'
Therefore I will boast all the more gladly about my weaknesses,
so that Christ's power may rest on me."
2 Corinthians 12:9

"Brothers and sisters, I do not consider myself yet to have taken hold of it. But one thing I do: Forgetting what is behind and straining toward what is ahead, I press on toward the goal to win the prize for which God has called me heavenward in Christ Jesus."
Philippians 3:13-14

"For I can do everything through Christ, who gives me strength."
Philippians 4:13

"Do not merely listen to the word,
and so deceive yourselves. Do what it says."
James 1:22

Scan the code with your mobile device for a prayer.

Wrap Up And Thank You

HOW TO CONNECT WITH US

Visit our website www.SpeakTIL.com
Join our email list for upcoming events and updates

Follow us on social media
Facebook: STIL Speak Truth in Love, Inc
Instagram: @speaktil

Schedule a virtual or in person retreat or training

Reach out to us for information or coaching
info@SpeakTIL.com
Wendy@SpeakTIL.com
Sarah@SpeakTIL.com

THANK YOU

for taking this journey with us to learn to Thrive in Life using God's word and His help. We hope you'll use this workbook as a living document that you can return to again and again, to help you connect with God, yourself, and others.

OUR PRAYER

'"The Lord bless you
and keep you;
the Lord make his face shine on you
and be gracious to you;
the Lord turn his face toward you
and give you peace."'
Numbers 6:24-26 (NIV)

Wendy and Sarah

STIL Speak Truth in Love, Inc.

VISION:
To empower people around the world to connect with God and His Word, and equip them in living a thriving life filled with purpose, hope, peace, and joy.

MISSION:
We provide globally accessible resources, trainings, and coaching that empower and equip people to live a purpose-filled life through a thriving relationship with God, themselves, and others.

CORE VALUES:
Joy, integrity, honesty, collaboration, family, unity, love, audacious generosity, and relationship.

Ingram Content Group UK Ltd.
Milton Keynes UK
UKHW050304250423
420701UK00009B/90